GW00417603

Personal Financial Planner

FINANCIAL TIMES
Prentice Hall

In an increasingly competitive world, it is quality
of thinking that gives an edge – an idea that opens new
doors, a technique that solves a problem, or an insight
that simply helps make sense of it all.

We work with leading authors in the fields of
management and finance to bring cutting-edge thinking
and best learning practice to a global market.

Under a range of leading imprints, including
Financial Times Prentice Hall, we create world-class
print publications and electronic products giving
readers knowledge and understanding which can then
be applied, whether studying or at work.

To find out more about our business and professional
products, you can visit us at www.business-minds.com

For other Pearson Education publications, visit
www.pearsoned-ema.com

Personal Financial Planner

*The indispensable tool for building financial
security and managing wealth*

Debbie Harrison

An imprint of Pearson Education

London • New York • San Francisco • Toronto • Sydney
Tokyo • Singapore • Hong Kong • Cape Town • Madrid
Paris • Milan • Munich • Amsterdam

PEARSON EDUCATION LIMITED

Head Office:
Edinburgh Gate
Harlow CM20 2JE
Tel: +44 (0)1279 623623
Fax: +44 (0)1279 431059

London Office:
128 Long Acre, London WC2E 9AN
Tel: +44 (0)20 7447 2000
Fax: +44 (0)20 7240 5771
Website: www.business-minds.com

First edition 1997
Revised edition 1999
Second edition first published in Great Britain 2002

ISBN 0 273 64364 9

British Library Cataloguing in Publication Data
A CIP catalogue record for this book can be obtained from the British Library.

10 9 8 7 6 5 4 3 2 1

Designed by designdeluxe, Bath
Typeset by Northern Phototypesetting Co. Ltd, Bolton
Printed and bound in Great Britain by Biddles Ltd, www.biddles.co.uk

The Publishers' policy is to use paper manufactured from sustainable forests.

About the author

Debbie Harrison is an award-winning financial author and journalist. She writes regularly for the *Financial Times* and is the author of five FT reports on retail and institutional investment. Her consumer books include *The First Time Investor*, *Pension Power* and *The Money Zone*, published by Pearson Education and *How to Make it in The City*, published by Virgin Publishing.

Contents

CONTENTS

Foreword

by Simon Pym Williamson,
President of the Institute of Financial Planning

What is financial planning?

The definition of financial planning used by the Institute of Financial Planning is as follows:

> *'Financial planning is a professional service for clients who need objective assistance in organizing their personal or corporate financial affairs to more readily achieve their goals.'*

You will notice that this definition makes no reference to financial products or to the sale of such products. The financial planner is there to help you identify the objectives you wish to achieve, and then to show you how these objectives might be best fulfilled. In practice, financial planners will strive to help you define, review and attain your financial objectives with less risk and cost than if you tried to do it yourself.

We can, therefore, clearly distinguish the provider of financial services from the financial planner as follows.

The provider of financial services is concerned with choosing the best or most appropriate products for your needs. The financial planner's concern is to identify and advise on the best solution to the overall management of your affairs.

The provider of a financial service is 'product orientated' and sells products. The financial planner is 'client orientated' and sells advice. In the UK at present, there are many providers of financial services, but relatively few financial planners.

The financial planner will take a comprehensive and strategic approach to your circumstances and will start by identifying your objectives and reviewing the strengths and weaknesses of your arrangements. This will not be confined to a single area of personal finance, but will cover all areas, including:

■ risk management
■ insurance

■ investment

■ retired estate planning including wills and trusts

■ school fee planning

■ taxation

■ cashflow planning

■ special needs including long-term healthcare.

The financial planner recognizes the inter-dependencies that connect all areas and will view the separate strands of your financial affairs as a total picture.

The financial planner, therefore, provides an identifiable professional service and is happy to call upon other expert professionals where their advice might be helpful or necessary. The planner is not in competition with other professions and therefore will be pleased to work with your existing professional advisers or to suggest appropriate firms if you require professional help.

The profession of financial planning has already attracted people from the related disciplines of accountancy, banking, insurance, taxation, stock-broking, education and the legal profession. Professional and well-qualified financial planners will have a broad depth of knowledge across all of these disciplines in order to provide their client with a holistic solution.

The process of financial planning

There are six main stages to personal financial planning:

■ Stage One – gathering data.

■ Stage Two – establishing your objectives and/or problems.

■ Stage Three – processing and analyzing information.

■ Stage Four – recommending a comprehensive plan.

■ Stage Five – implementing the plan.

■ Stage Six – monitoring the plan.

The description of financial planning as a six-stage process is a helpful model, but like all models, an over-simplification of the actual process. The stages in practice do not necessarily follow in clear-cut sequence. For example, frequent processing and analysis of information will require the planner to reconsider your objectives.

It is important to appreciate that financial planning is a continuous process. The plan has to be updated and modified to allow for changes in the financial environment or in your personal circumstances.

A professional financial planner will address your overall needs and those of any other people directly affected by your plan. Planners deliberately divorce their planning and advice services from recommendations relating to financial products. Some planners offer their clients the option of purchasing essential financial products as a completely separate step, perhaps even with an unconnected third party. In this case they charge fees for their services. Others will arrange products and offset commissions against fees payable.

For this reason most financial planners prefer to offer their advice on a fee basis. In this way you can be confident that you are paying for a service which is not linked or dependent on the sale of a product.

In conclusion, financial planners are qualified to give professional advice on a broad range of subjects and to introduce specialist expertise where necessary. Your planner will play a central role in the successful achievement of your goals.

Simon Pym Williamson CFP ALIA (dip)
Certified Financial Planner
President of the Institute of Financial Planning

Preface

Strange as it may seem, a different outcome in the May 2001 election would have had little impact on the way we run our personal finances. Behind the scenes both major political parties are united in their view that the state should provide a safety net for the very needy and everyone else should be financially self-sufficient.

This means we should address our financial needs for key areas such as protection insurances, pensions, mortgages and further education for our children. There is no magic one-size-fits-all solution, but despite what the cynics say, a little knowledge goes a very long way towards avoiding expensive mistakes.

Protection insurance

The state provides very little if your earnings stop as a result of sickness, long-term disability or even death. Unfortunately, an increasing number of employers are also opting out of private welfare and are either leaving it entirely up to you or providing the very minimum with a range of optional extras through a flexible benefits package at work. Some are offering what are known as voluntary benefits, where the employer negotiates cut-price premiums but you foot the bill.

At the same time there are hordes of eager salesmen out there anxious to sell you the latest all-singing and all-dancing protection products. Some of these are first class, others are rubbish. Many are not even covered by the financial services regulators. You need to know what you require to protect your family and how to get the best price and level of service.

Pension planning

Since the last edition of this book was published we have seen further evidence of the necessity for robust financial planning. In particular in April 2001 the first stakeholder pension schemes were launched. Contrary to popular opinion a stakeholder is not a new product but is simply a personal pension that must guarantee to offer low costs, easy access (for example you can contribute as little as £20 per month) and penalty-free entry and exit terms.

These schemes are designed to fill the gap in private pension provision for the millions of workers who do not have access to a company scheme and for whom personal pensions have proved expensive and inflexible.

At present if you do not contribute to a company scheme it is not compulsory to make other provisions. But at some point in the future the government is almost certain to introduce compulsion in order to ensure we save enough for our retirement. New rules make it a lot easier for everyone to save up to £3,600 a year in a tax-efficient pension plan – and this includes non-earners, not just those in paid employment. The choice of plans, however, is bewildering and this is where we intend to help you.

Stakeholder schemes also herald a range of new tax planning opportunities. The break with the earnings link makes the stakeholder annual contribution a universal allowance similar to the £7,000 annual individual savings account (Isa). This means that you can put aside money for a non-working spouse and for your children.

The introduction of stakeholder schemes coincides with radical changes to the state pensions. The basic pension has been underpinned with a minimum income guarantee, but the earnings-related second state pension is going to disappear shortly and will be replaced by a flat-rate benefit available only to those whose income is too low to save privately. These changes are important and you need to know your rights in order to make the most of existing benefits.

The cost of further education

There's no such thing as a free lunch – or free education for that matter. Higher education is open to everyone, provided you can pay. These days saving and borrowing is the name of the game and good old-fashioned grants are a thing of the past.

If you want your kids to go to college or university, it is likely to cost about £7,000 a year – more if the college is in London. Your kids can borrow the money but many parents who enjoyed debt-free student days would like their offspring to do the same. So, even those who have avoided school fees now have some serious financial planning to do.

There is nothing magic about a school fees or university fees plan – it's just a question of saving the right amounts and getting the cash flow sorted so that the investments mature when the fees fall due. This book shows you how.

Mortgages

The mis-selling of endowment mortgages has created considerable unease among homeowners who relied on financial salesmen to recommend the right investment to repay their mortgage – and in thousands of cases were led up the garden path.

The financial services regulators always seem to be one step behind the cowboys and are tackling this latest scandal while they are still mopping up the dregs of the personal pension mis-selling affair.

If, like many investors, you are wondering just how to find the right mortgage and the best investment to back it, you will find in these pages some genuinely unbiased advice and a wealth of tips on how to get the best deals.

Long-term care

The good news is that we are living longer. The bad news is that our final years tend to be unhealthy ones and we often require residential or nursing home accommodation. This is extraordinarily expensive and without careful planning can eat into the very savings you were hoping to pass on to your children. In this new edition we look at government policy on the cost of long-term care and show you how to plan for this event.

Volatile markets

Over the past five years it has become increasingly easy to invest your money in a wide range of collective funds or even directly in equities and bonds. The availability of online research, fund supermarkets and execution-only stockbrokers on the Net has revolutionized the way we can invest spare capital. What it hasn't done is made it any less risky.

Indeed, there appears to be an inverse correlation between the ease with which we can part with our money and the jitteriness of world capital markets. Anyone with money invested in equities – and particularly those who went into technology stocks – will have suffered poor and possibly negative returns.

Fortunately – or unfortunately, depending on your point of view – financial institutions and advisers are always coming up with new ways to cushion the impact of volatility. 'With profits' funds, guaranteed funds (backed by financial instruments known as derivatives) and the latest – hedge funds – are all designed to prevent the value of your investment from plummeting when markets go through the floor.

As an investor you need to be aware of the way these black-box products work because they tend to be extremely complicated and have at least one significant drawback that may not be made clear in the sales process. In many cases the salespeople themselves will not understand how the products work.

This book helps you to appreciate the fundamentals of investing so that you can select the right types of assets and the right types of products for your requirements and your risk tolerance.

Caveat emptor – buyer beware – is as important today as it ever was.

Debbie Harrison

Introduction

The era of the welfare state has passed and it is increasingly clear that the key to financial security lies in the hands of the individual, not the government. For some, this will be a welcome challenge. For others, it will be a daunting responsibility.

Whether you view the subject of finance with enthusiasm or trepidation, this book is for you. Financial planning is about setting the right goals for your circumstances, and building up a well-integrated package of insurances, investments and taxation arrangements to meet those goals.

Step 1: Find the right adviser

Clearly, the success of your financial plan will depend largely on the competence of your chosen adviser. But finding the right firm will not prove easy. There are literally thousands of so-called financial advisers out there, ranging from the fully qualified, fee-based professionals to the archetypal insurance salesman whose only hope of earning a crust is to persuade you to buy a policy you probably don't need, or an investment plan which combines the twin evils of lousy performance and high charges.

To save you a lot of time and money, this book explains how to find a good firm of advisers. Here you will learn how the advice channels in the UK operate, what questions to ask, what qualifications to look for, and what research and information technology a good adviser should have. Moreover, since the financial services regulators do not provide a list of 'jolly good' advisers, we show you how to draw up your own from a tried and tested shortlist of organizations dedicated to good-quality, independent financial advice.

Admittedly, no system is 100 per cent foolproof. If you do feel you have been hoodwinked into buying the wrong insurance policy or investing in an inappropriate fund, we also explain how to make a successful complaint and who to turn to for help.

Step 2: Protect your family

The best-laid plans to generate a good income for your family from earnings and investments will come to nothing if you do not protect your chief sources of revenue in the event of your death or serious illness. For this reason, before we look at investments, Section 2 of this book deals with the essential protection insurances.

Many of these products are complicated and riddled with small print. Most are not regulated by the Financial Services Act. When disaster strikes you could find out too late that the small-print exclusions render the policy worthless. Section 2, therefore, will help you assess the levels of cover you need and determine which type of policy suits your circumstances. We explain how to get the best from:

■ life assurance

■ income protection plans (lump-sum and regular-income)

■ mortgage payment protection plans

■ private medical insurance

■ long-term care for the elderly.

Throughout we highlight the pitfalls and the most important policy terms, so you can avoid the products and providers whose only guarantee is that you will be let down in an emergency.

Step 3: Taxation

Before you embark on your tax-efficient investment planning we draw your attention to the most important tax matters. Tax planning is not an isolated exercise but an integral element in your overall financial plan. For this reason, taxation is dealt with at various stages throughout this book as it affects your insurance and investment decisions. In addition you need to understand how to get the best value from your annual allowances and exemptions, how income and capital gains tax work, and how you can avoid inheritance tax.

Don't forget the old adage – 'Where there's a will there's a relative'. Two in three people do not have a will, and as a result impose unnecessary administration and costs on their families and have no control over the choice of beneficiaries. This section explains the importance of making a will and highlights the main points this document must cover.

Step 4: Successful investing

Once you have dealt with protection insurance and taxation you can turn to savings and investment. This section will help you understand risk, return, the most important asset classes, and how to use them to achieve your short-, medium- and long-term investment goals. It will also help you decide whether to invest directly in equities and bonds or via collective funds which spread risk and offer economies of scale. Armed with this vital information you can sift through the chapters which follow, make your choice and find out how to buy, monitor and sell your investments. We include:

- deposits and comparatively 'safe' investments such as cash, Individual savings accounts (Isas), National Savings, gilts (held to maturity) and guaranteed income bonds
- unit trusts, investment trusts and open-ended investment companies
- equity-based individual savings accounts
- life assurance investments
- direct investment in equities, gilts and bonds.

Step 5: Long-term investment goals – mortgages and education

Although part of your overall investment strategy, your mortgage and, where applicable, your children's education costs are likely to be your largest liabilities throughout your working life. Section 5 explains how to define your mortgage requirements and set sensible debt limits. We also explain how the different types of mortgage work, including:

- repayment mortgages
- endowment mortgages
- Isa mortgages
- pension mortgages
- the bells and whistles: fixed-rate, discounts, low-start
- the sting in the tail: the penalties you may face if you want to switch to a different type of mortgage or want to pay off your debt early
- home income plans.

For some parents, private schooling is an essential requirement. It can start from as early as age 2 or 3 when the children attend private nurseries, and can continue to age 22 or 23 if the children go to university. Remember, even if you manage to send your children to a good state school, the chances are you will qualify for very little, if any, help towards further education. The cost is phenomenal and few parents can afford to fund the entire bill direct from income. Part of the cost must be derived from a sensible investment portfolio. Section 5 provides all the information you need to get started on your education fees plan, including:

- the choice of school
- state assistance, scholarships and grants
- special fee schemes
- the cost of higher education
- investment plans
- insurance
- organizations worth contacting.

Step 6: Your pension

Over 10 million employees and their dependants rely on occupational pension schemes for their financial security in retirement, and for important family protection insurances during their working lives. A further 8 million are covered by individual plans, while thousands of small businesses and partnerships operate pension schemes which in some cases are unique to the UK.

But all pensions are not equal and for the same level of contributions, different schemes and plans will produce very different results. This section tells you how to spot the difference. We examine:

- state pensions
- the new stakeholder schemes
- company pension schemes
- topping up your company scheme
- special schemes for higher earners
- personal pensions
- annuities.

Guide to the organizations and the jargon

Finally, in Appendices 1, 2 and 3 we provide a glossary of financial jargon, contact details for the most important organizations, a guide to making complaints, and a run-down of Internet services.

Author's notes

Throughout this book, unless stated otherwise, the male gender is used to denote both male and female.

The professional firms of financial planners can also be described as financial advisers, but there are many 'advisers' who certainly could not be described as professional financial planners. The important difference between planners and advisers is explained in the Foreword and in Section 1, but elsewhere, for the sake of simplicity, the book uses 'adviser' as a generic descriptive term.

Acknowledgements

Many people helped with this book and the source of specific material is provided in the text. I would like to thank in particular the Institute for Financial Planning, plus the following organizations: Barclays Capital, the Council of Mortgage Lenders, the Financial Services Authority, the Independent Schools Information Service, ProShare and the Tunbridge Wells Equitable Friendly Society.

Call on the experts

How to find a good financial planner

The UK has more than 27,000 'independent financial advisers', several thousand more professional advisers and a further 70,000 company representatives. Trying to find a good firm may resemble an exercise involving a large haystack and a very small needle. In practice, however, it is possible to eliminate most of this army of advisers by considering carefully what *you want*, not what *they sell*.

Some of the best advisers in the UK are more correctly described as 'financial planners'. Don't worry too much about the labels, but do focus on the range of advice, the qualifications and experience of your adviser.

What is financial planning?

Financial planners take what they call an 'holistic' or integrated approach to your financial affairs. The reasons for this integrated approach are obvious when you consider the following 'shopping list', typical of most families' financial requirements:

- protection insurances (life assurance, income protection, mortgage protection)
- general investments and savings
- retirement provision (state, company and private pensions)
- funding for major liabilities (investing for specific items such as school fees and mortgages)
- income and capital gains tax planning
- estate planning (passing on your wealth, inheritance tax planning, making a will).

Each item has an impact on one or more of the other categories, so rather than deal with your mortgage or your pension in isolation, financial planners would tackle them in the light of all your investments, tax and insurance needs.

Who are the financial planners?

Although financial planners have been around for a long time, it is only fairly recently that they have adopted a higher profile and recognizable identity which distinguishes them from other advisers. This is partly due to the greater involvement in financial services of the professional firms – in particular the accountants and solicitors, who represent about 50 per cent of the financial planners.

A good firm of financial planners will have access to a wide range of technical expertise, covering everything from protection insurance and taxation to general savings and specific investments for pensions, mortgages and school fees. If the firm is too small to cater for all these requirements, it should have a close working relationship with other professional firms which can supply the missing elements. In order to provide the best financial plan, firms must be able to draw on every available good-quality insurance product, savings scheme and taxation arrangement. Above all, they should not be influenced by the amount of sales commission offered by the product providers.

But before looking at who can give you advice, it is helpful to understand the system of regulation in the UK and how it protects you.

Authorization and regulation

Under the Financial Services Act it is a criminal offence to give investment advice without being authorized. Unfortunately the regulatory system has been widely criticized for being too slow. Several mainstream investments – personal pensions, endowment mortgages and home income plans, for example – have been the subject of a major mis-selling scandal. Caveat emptor – buyer beware – is as important today as it ever was.

FINANCIAL SNAPSHOT

The term 'financial adviser' is a bit like 'consultant' and 'engineer'. It can mean a one-man band which sells everything from motor insurance to mortgages, to well-resourced, qualified professional firms of stockbrokers, chartered accountants, actuaries and solicitors.

Financial Services Authority (FSA)

There are three main investment watchdogs, which are currently being combined under the Financial Services Authority. The FSA is the designated agency to which Parliament has delegated many of the powers under the Financial Services Act 1986. The FSA reports directly to the government (HM Treasury) and has statutory powers to enforce its requirements and decisions.

The Financial Services Act makes it a criminal offence to undertake investment business without being either authorized to do so or exempt under the Act. Authorization is normally obtained from one of the three front-line regulators – IMRO, SFA and PIA (see below). The main exception is professional firms whose business inevitably includes some investment business – for instance, accountants or solicitors. In this case authorization is provided by their professional body.

Each watchdog is responsible for regulating different types of investment business.

■ The Investment Management Regulatory Organisation (IMRO) regulates those: managing investments; acting as a manager or trustee of authorized unit trust schemes; managing or operating other collective investment schemes; giving investment advice to institutional investors.

■ The Securities and Futures Authority (SFA) regulates stockbrokers dealing in shares, options, and financial and commodities futures.

■ The Personal Investment Authority (PIA) regulates firms that advise, market and sell investments to private investors.

In May 1997 the government announced its intention to create a single financial services regulator, replacing the framework of statutory and self-regulation established by the Financial Services Act. In June 1998, responsibility for the financial regulation of banks was transferred from the Bank of England to the FSA, and the majority of IMRO and other self-regulatory organization staff transferred to FSA contracts of employment.

The process of authorization

To be authorized, organizations must demonstrate that they are and will remain fit and proper persons to undertake investment business of the kind proposed. The 'fit and proper' test encompasses:

■ the honesty and integrity of the organization, its directors, managers, staff and any controlling shareholders

- the experience, qualifications and competence of its management
- the adequacy of its financial resources
- its ability to conduct investment business of the kind proposed honestly, fairly and competently
- its ability to comply with the regulator's rules.

The organization must establish systems to ensure all the rules are followed, to report key facts to the regulator and to report regularly on its financial welfare. It must be ready to co-operate with any request for information or any investigation. Finally, it must accept it is subject to the disciplinary system of the regulator and must pay its share of the regulation costs.

The Act covers every firm or company providing investment advice or an investment service. If someone gives you advice on products covered by the Act and is not himself authorized, he is breaking the law. Check authorization by calling the FSA, which runs a comprehensive database. See Appendix II.

Bear in mind that not everything sold as an 'investment' has to be authorized. For example, tangible assets directly purchased – gold coins, rare stamps, antiques, vintage cars and wines, for example – are not classed as investments under the Act.

As a rule of thumb you can regard an 'investment' as a non-tangible asset. The Act's definition of 'investments' includes shares, debentures and other securities (government securities or 'gilts' for example), certain options and warrants, unit trusts and other forms of collective investments, futures contracts and some long-term life assurance contracts. 'Investment business' includes dealing, arranging deals in, managing and advising on investments, as well as setting up and operating collective investments. Investment business is distinguished from deposit-taking business, which is covered by the Banking Act and the Building Societies Act.

> **Bear in mind that not everything sold as an 'investment' has to be authorized.**

This may all seem rather academic but the point is this: *If you buy something which is not covered by the Act, the FSA regulators cannot investigate your case and you are not entitled to compensation if things go wrong*.

Who gives the advice?

Under the FSA, advisers are split into two broad categories: 'representatives' of a company and 'independent financial advisers'. It may be possible in future for sales staff to represent a limited number of companies for certain products – which will add to the confusion no end.

Representatives

Company representatives (also known as 'direct salesmen' and 'tied agents') are employed by – and work solely for – just one company. Their income consists of a basic salary and a commission element. Some representatives are remunerated purely by sales commission which means if they don't sell you a policy, they don't eat. Fortunately, an increasing number of representatives receive quite decent basic salaries, so there is less need for them to verbally beat you into submission. Where commission is paid, the total bill will depend on the level of premium or contribution, whether this is a one-off or a regular investment contract, and the investment period.

Buying direct from a company is not necessarily a bad thing. Some of the best insurance and investment products – as well as some of the worst – are sold in this way. The important point to remember is that this type of adviser is permitted by law to sell only the products of the company he represents and through which he is authorized. You might be lucky and pick a winner, but unless you are prepared to thoroughly research the market for the best combination of charges, potential investment returns and flexibility, frankly, buying direct is a gamble.

Appointed representatives are companies which have a contract with a financial institution to sell one or more of their products in return for commission. The appointed representative is not necessarily employed or owned by the institution and, confusingly, may act independently in other lines of business.

A typical example is a building society which conducts a full range of its own mortgage facilities but sells the endowment, personal equity plan or personal pension products of one life company only (often its own). So, if you want an Isa mortgage, you will borrow XYZ Building Society's money, but there will be no choice of Isa products – you will have to take the ABC Company's Isa – or go elsewhere.

The appointed representative, like the company representative, is not obliged to tell you how competitive the products he sells are in terms of charges and performance.

Independent financial advisers

Independent financial advisers (IFAs) are not tied to one company. Their job is to examine your needs and to search the market for the product that offers the best value in terms of performance, charges, and contract flexibility, among other factors.

In theory at least, you stand a better chance of coming away with the right insurances and investments than if you go to a company or appointed representative. However, the term 'independent' is not synonymous with 'expert'. IFAs vary considerably in their level of competence.

How to make your choice

Your choice of adviser will be dictated partly by your pocket and partly by your requirements. However, there are certain features worth checking.

Qualifications

Qualifications are becoming increasingly important in the financial services sector and are a good indication of a firm's commitment to high standards. If you are interested in direct equity investment as well as collective funds, you probably need the services of an investment manager or stockbroker. Stockbrokers are regulated by the Securities and Futures Authority (SFA) and in order to give you advice they must first pass the SFA's 'Registered Persons Examinations'.

A committed investment adviser is also likely to be a member of The Securities Institute. To become a full member the adviser needs to pass the Institute's Diploma, which is a professional-level qualification for practitioners who have already gained experience in such areas as securities, derivatives, corporate finance and investment management.

> If you are interested in direct equity investment as well as collective funds, you probably need the services of an investment manager or stockbroker.

For more general investment advice, you can go to a firm of independent financial advisers or financial planners. This category includes an increasing number of chartered accountants and solicitors who specialize in this area.

By the end of June 1997, all advisers had to achieve a 'benchmark' or basic qualification. There are several of these, but you are most likely to come across the Financial Planning Certificate (FPC). This is examined by the Chartered Insurance Institute (CII). The Securities Institute also runs a benchmark exam for independent advisers – the Investment Advice Certificate. Accountants and bankers have their own benchmark regulatory qualifications.

The next stage up from the FPC is the Advanced Financial Planning Certificate (AFPC), which includes a personal investment planning syllabus. The AFPC allows advisers to become full members of the Society of Financial Advisers (SOFA) – the financial services arm of the CII. SOFA has also launched associate and fellowship qualifications.

The AFPC also allows advisers to become associate members of the Institute of Financial Planning (IFP). Through the Institute, members can acquire Certified Financial Planner status, which is recognized in other countries, including the UK, US, Canada, Japan, Australia and New

Zealand. One of the UK's top qualifications for planners/advisers is the IFP fellowship exam. All of the fellows are fee-based and independent.

Paying for advice

Stockbroker/investment manager charges include commissions which are charged on purchase or sale of securities – usually a percentage of the money invested. Alternatively, the firm may charge a fee once or twice a year for a continuing investment management service. Some firms use a combination of both fee and dealing commissions.

Other professional advisers – accountants and solicitors for example – are fee-based and any sales commission would be offset against fees or re-invested in your plan. The broader band of independent financial advisers may operate on a fee basis or accept commission. Some do both.

Fee-based advisers charge anything from around £50–£300 per hour depending on whether you go to a local high street adviser or a leading firm of consulting actuaries or chartered accountants. As a rough guide, however, for good advice you can expect to pay at least £80–£130 per hour.

One of the particularly daft aspects of the tax system is that you pay fees out of your taxed income, on top of which you have to pay VAT. If you pay through the commission route, not only do you avoid VAT, but in the case of pension plans, effectively you get tax relief at your highest rate on the payment. This is because the commission is deducted from your pension contributions, which themselves benefit from full tax relief.

Commission and flexibility

Investment companies are required by the financial services regulators to disclose all their charges in full, including sales commission, in a pre-sale 'key features' document.

Commission rates vary depending on the size of premium and the term of the contract. As a rough guide you can assume that on a 'single premium' or one-off payment to a pension or life assurance investment plan, the sales commission will be 4–6 per cent of your investment. For a 25-year 'regular premium' plan, where you agree to pay a certain amount each month or each year, the commission could be worth about 70 per cent of the value of your first year's contributions.

Now, over the long term there is very little difference between the total commission cost for a regular premium plan and a plan where you pay in the same amount but your contributions are classed as a series of single premiums. However, regular premium plans can be inflexible. This is because many life and pension companies, particularly the direct sales operations, pay advisers upfront all of the commission that would otherwise have been paid over the entire investment period. This means that if you pull out in the early years you will have very little to show for your money.

If you do buy commission-based products, your best bet is to ask for single premium or 'recurring' single premium terms. Under this system, each contribution is treated as a one-off, and only the commission related to that amount is paid to the adviser. However, to encourage regular savers, some companies have low charges on regular premium contracts, so do ask before signing up.

Impact of charges on your fund

Your adviser will give you a pre-sale 'key features' document which shows what your fund would be worth at different stages during the investment period, assuming a certain growth rate. The purpose of this is to show you the impact of the companies' charges on your returns. This can be used to compare different companies' charges to check if you are getting good value for money. As a quick guide, refer to the 'reduction in growth' figure which shows by how much the charges would reduce the annual yield.

> If your investment company turns out to be one of the worst performers in its category, it is little comfort to know that the charges are modest.

A low reduction in growth figure for one level of contribution does not indicate that charges are low across the board. Different charges apply to different premium levels and the effect of a flat-rate monthly fee, for example, will be proportionately greater on lower premiums.

Charges are important but should not be the sole selection criterion. If your investment company turns out to be one of the worst performers in its category, it is little comfort to know that the charges are modest.

The client agreement

If you plan to use your adviser on a regular basis, you should have a written agreement which sets out the firm's terms and what services it will provide. A clearly worded client agreement gives you a benchmark against which you can judge the adviser's performance, particularly where the firm has direct responsibility for investing your money.

The following checklist includes the main points in a client agreement. You should add any further points that apply to your particular circumstances.

- The regulation of the adviser under the Financial Services Act 1986.

- Which services this entitles the adviser to carry out and the services it is not authorised to undertake. For example, is the adviser authorized to hold client money?

- Permission (required by the Consumer Credit Act 1974) for the adviser to act on your behalf to negotiate mortgages, loans and overdrafts.

- The period of agreement and period of notice on both sides (usually a minimum of 30 days).

- Your responsibility to provide the information the adviser needs. (For example, to give appropriate advice, your adviser needs a clear idea of your existing investments and your attitude to risk.)

- Details of access to your other advisers, for example your bank manager, accountant and pension provider.

- Your right to veto any recommendations.

- A confidentiality clause.

- Details of how your documents will be stored.

- Fee rates per hour for different levels of advisers within the firm and details of any due dates for regular fees.

- Details of VAT likely to be charged.

- Treatment of commissions if the adviser acts on a fee basis – for example, does the firm re-invest this money or offset it against fees.

- Treatment of complaints and disputes.

Changing your financial adviser

If you already have a financial adviser but you are not fully satisfied with the service, you should consider changing to a more professional firm. This can save you money as well as ensure a higher level of regular servicing for your investments and insurances.

The advent of financial adviser websites has taken a lot of the legwork out of the selection process. However, if the transition to the new firm is not handled carefully you could end up paying unnecessary charges on old or duplicate policies.

By the time you realize you need a new and better adviser you are likely to have collected a lot of financial baggage. In the real world, before we take financial planning seriously, most of us accumulate an unco-ordinated assortment of investments and insurance plans sold by an even less co-ordinated range of financial institutions and advisers.

Your new adviser can't plan for your goals if he does not know where you are now, so one of his first jobs is to evaluate what you have got already so that he can prepare a full fact find. To do this he will need to contact all of your existing providers and notify them that the new firm has taken over as your adviser. At the same time your new adviser will send a pro forma to providers to get an up-to-date picture of the terms and conditions of your insurance policies and investment plans.

Many people accumulate duplicate pension plans and insurance policies. One planner we spoke to said a particular client who joined him had 17 different pension policies and didn't really know why. Overall he was paying about the right amount in pension contributions for his age and earnings, but the cost in policy fees and commissions was excessive, to put it mildly.

A professional adviser's aim will be to get everything together in a single clear schedule. You have the right to request copies of all your documents from your existing adviser, but if there is anything missing you or your new adviser might have to go direct to the provider.

When you transfer the agency agreement to the new firm you need to discuss how your adviser is to be remunerated. With most insurance policies and regular premium investments the provider is likely to pay a commission to your existing adviser. The simplest way to deal with this is to transfer the commission payments to your new adviser who will accept this as part of the overall remuneration if the firm works on a commission basis, or offset it against fees.

What you can't do is reinvest the commission in the investment plan once it is established on a commission-paying basis. This is not the fault of the adviser. Insurance companies in particular have notoriously archaic systems designed to deduct commissions for advisers from your premiums. Once a plan or policy is set up on this basis it is virtually impossible to change it.

For the same reasons, if you dismiss an adviser and deal with an insurance company directly, in most cases you will not benefit from the reduced costs. Instead the insurance company will pocket the commission it would otherwise have paid to your adviser.

In the terms of business client agreement your new adviser should explain its services clearly and set out the level and method of charging. Don't entrust the adviser with anything until you have signed this agreement (see above). This is your assurance that the firm will act within the guidelines and boundaries agreed and if it fails to do so the agreement provides you with access to redress and eligibility to the investor's compensation scheme (ICS).

For your financial planner to achieve the best results, they need to be in contact with your other professional advisers. For example your solicitor should be involved in estate planning, while your accountant needs to keep your planner up to date with your tax affairs in order to make the most of your allowances and exemptions. This is particularly important in the area of pension planning where contributions are directly linked to annual earnings (apart from the new stakeholder schemes, which are discussed on page 181).

Summary

- ■ Unless you are sure of your ability to research the market thoroughly, seek *independent* advice.
- ■ Check in particular the level of qualifications held by the staff and the firm's research resources.
- ■ Ideally pay for your advice by fees rather than commission, as this removes any potential bias in the firm's recommendations.

Glossary of terms

Company and appointed representatives advise on the products of just one company.

Independent financial advisers should consider all the products and investments available and select the best for your circumstances.

Further information

For a list of regulators, professional bodies and adviser organizations, see Appendix 2. For a guide to making a complaint, see Appendix 2.

Protection comes first

Protect your family if you die

If you die, your family gets very little from the state. Therefore if you have any dependants who would suffer financially as a result of your death, you need life assurance. Fortunately this is relatively cheap and easy to buy.

The 'sum assured' – that is the amount of cover you take out – should do two things:

■ It should repay any outstanding loans including the mortgage, and

■ It should allow your family to maintain its standard of living by replacing your income in full or by topping up any other benefits you may receive.

How much do you need?

The amount of cover you buy must be geared to your liabilities. As a rough guide, you could multiply your salary by 10 to provide a lump sum for your dependants which, when invested, would generate a reasonable replacement annual income. A more precise method is to calculate the income you actually need to meet expenditure, including the cost of outstanding loans.

Consider carefully the period you need to insure. One way of looking at this is to cover the period during which any borrowing remains outstanding,

F I N A N C I A L   S N A P S H O T

Women tend to live longer than men, so generally can expect to pay less for their life assurance policies than a man of the same age, because there is less chance the insurance company will have to pay up.

and until the children have ceased to be dependent – up to age 23 if you expect them to go to university. However, more wealthy individuals who plan to retire early should provide cover until earnings stop and pensions start. Don't forget that where there are young children, the partner responsible for childcare must also be insured. The cost of a full-time nanny could easily run to £8,000–£10,000 a year.

The basic calculation, then, is 'income requirement plus debt minus any existing cover'. Existing cover may be provided by your company pension scheme or other private insurances. Pension schemes can provide up to four times the level of your annual salary as a tax-free cash lump sum if you die. They should also provide a spouse's pension and possibly a pension for your children if they are under 18.

Personal pension plans also provide life cover. However, in this case, the value will not be linked to your salary, but instead will depend on how much is in your fund. If you have only recently started a pension plan, this could be very little, so you will need to pay for extra life assurance while your fund is building up. You can also use up to 5 per cent of your personal pension contribution allowance to pay for life assurance. However, you may need to pay maximum contributions to your pension, so think carefully before you use this option.

The main drawback with life assurance linked to your company pension scheme is that it applies only while you are working and contributing. If you are in this position, make the most of it while it lasts, but be prepared to top up with private insurance if your employment circumstances change.

In particular, make sure the cover provided by your old and new jobs overlaps. A common mistake is to go off for a holiday between jobs and to forget to arrange stopgap insurance.

> The two simplest products are **level term assurance** and **family income benefit**. The term assurance lump sum can be invested to provide an annual income and/or used to pay off debt, while family income benefit can directly replace the shortfall in annual income.

Which type of policy?

Once you identify the shortfall in your provision, you can use one of the methods listed below to fill the gap.

The two simplest products are **level term assurance** and **family income benefit**. The term assurance lump sum can be invested to provide an annual income and/or used to pay off debt, while family income benefit can directly replace the shortfall in annual income.

Most life assurance policies work on the 'you drop dead, we pay up' principle. However, some companies offer **whole of life** plans which combine insurance and investment by deducting the cost of life cover from your savings plan.

The following descriptions explain your basic options.

Level term assurance

Level term assurance provides a tax-free cash lump sum if you die within the period insured. However, if you die the day after the term expires, you get nothing. Unless the policy is assigned to cover a specific liability – for example your mortgage debt – it is sensible to write it under trust, so that the lump sum does not form part of your estate if you die. In this way, the policy proceeds could be passed on to your children, for example, without having to wait for probate to be granted to your executors (see Chapter 7).

Life assurance can be written on a single or joint life basis. A joint life policy covers more than one person – typically a husband and wife. It may be written to pay out if just one of the spouses dies ('joint life first death') or only when both have died ('joint life second death'). Experts reckon it is usually better – and only slightly more expensive – to arrange individual policies.

Remember, wherever you share ownership, you have an insurable interest, so it is important to take appropriate cover. Young people often buy houses together to share the cost, while older couples may purchase a holiday home with friends.

Term assurance comes in other forms.

- **Convertible renewable** term assurance gives you the right to extend the insurance period without further medical underwriting or, in some cases, to convert to an investment-linked plan. The former can be useful if you need to increase your life cover when you are older. Generally you would be asked to undergo a medical, and could pay much higher premiums if you are not in good health.

- **Decreasing** term assurance reduces at regular intervals and can be used to protect a debt which reduces in a similar way – for example, where the outstanding debt decreases over the loan period at regular intervals. However, repayment mortgage protection insurance is structured in a slightly different way to accommodate the specific pattern of the capital debt reduction (see page 132).

Decreasing term assurance can also be used as a means of covering an inheritance tax (IHT) liability where you have transferred assets to someone other than your spouse (known as a 'potentially exempt transfer') and there would be a reducing IHT liability if you died during the seven years following the transfer. Remember, the insurance need only cover the potential tax liability – that is, a maximum of 40 per cent of the asset value in excess of £242,000 (in 2001–2002) – not the whole of the gift.

■ **Increasing** term assurance automatically increases the level of cover – usually in line with retail price inflation or a fixed amount – (say, 5 per cent) – without further medical underwriting. If you opt for this type of insurance, your annual premiums will also increase.

■ **Personal pension** term assurance is available to the self-employed and employees not in company schemes. Premiums attract full tax relief, provided they fall within your overall annual contribution limits. However, if you stop earning, you must also stop the plan. As mentioned above, although you can use up to 5 per cent of your annual pension contribution allowance to pay for life assurance, you may not want to do so if you need to pay the maximum amount to your pension plan.

Family income benefit

Family income benefit (FIB) provides a regular income from the date of death until the end of the insurance period. Tax treatment is favourable, because although the proceeds are paid in the form of a regular monthly income, technically they are classed as capital, so there is no income tax to pay. You can arrange for the income to remain the same ('level') or to increase each year. FIB is particularly useful where you have a young family and you want to insure the life of the spouse who stays at home to look after the children, so if he or she dies you can afford to employ a nanny and/or continue the school fees payments.

Whole of life plans

Whole of life plans, as the name suggests, pay a benefit whenever you die: there is no specific term. Given the certainty that the policy must pay out at some point, naturally the premiums tend to be higher than for term assurance. Whole of life policies combine insurance and investment. Your monthly premiums are invested and from this fund the insurance company deducts the amounts necessary to provide the life cover. When you die you get the fund value or the sum assured, whichever is greater. One common use for this type of policy is to provide a lump sum to cover your inheritance tax liability when you die.

Tips on buying your insurance

As a general rule, it is better to avoid products that combine insurance and investment. If what you need is a sensible amount of life cover, then simple term assurance is likely to offer the best value. If you want to build up some capital for your dependants, you could, for example, invest in tax-efficient Individual savings accounts (Isa) and take out a decreasing term assurance plan to provide a lump sum if you die early before your fund has had the chance to build up.

The premium you pay for your insurance will depend on your age, sex and your state of health, among other factors. You have a duty to complete the proposal form honestly and accurately. If you are considerably overweight or you smoke, your premiums may be 'loaded' – in other words, you pay more because there is a greater chance of an early death. Certain dangerous sports will also raise eyebrows in the underwriting department, and in turn may raise your premiums. In some cases your policy may not cover you while you indulge in these activities.

The proposal form will also ask if you have ever been tested for HIV (AIDS). If you are a single man and want a substantial amount of cover, you will probably be requested to complete a 'lifestyle' questionnaire which is designed to discover whether your private life exposes you to a higher than average risk of AIDS or other sexual diseases.

> You have a duty to complete the proposal form honestly and accurately. If you are considerably overweight or you smoke, your premiums may be 'loaded' – in other words you pay more because there is a greater chance of an early death.

The medical

Both men and women who want to take out a large amount of cover should expect to undergo a medical examination. Despite the aversion most people have to this, it does actually work in your favour. Where policies are not fully medically underwritten (this is usually the case with policies sold by direct mail or through off-the-page advertising), the under-writers assume there will be a much greater incidence of claims, so the premiums may be much higher than a medically underwritten contract.

The premium will also depend on the company. Life assurance is a very competitive market, which is why independent advice is essential. These days a good adviser will have access to a comprehensive database which will enable him to select the right features and the best rates available at any given time.

Your adviser should also make sure your premium rate is guaranteed. The cheapest rates are often offered by companies which reserve the right to 'review' premiums at any time. With reviewable premiums, effectively you are writing the insurance company a blank cheque.

How to pay

You may be offered a choice of payment options – for example, you could pay annually by cheque, or monthly by direct debit. Direct debit is probably the safest method, because the payments are guaranteed. If by mistake you overlook a reminder for your annual cheque, your cover may lapse, and if you have to re-apply, you may find that rates have increased due to you being older or a change in your health.

Life assurance as investments

Many companies sell investment plans which offer an element of life assurance. For details, see Chapter 11.

Summary

- If you have dependants who would suffer financially if you die, you need life assurance.
- As a rough guide to how much cover to take out, multiply your salary by 10, add in the value of any outstanding loans and deduct any existing cover, for example from a company pension scheme.
- Don't forget to top up your life assurance if your company benefits package changes when you switch jobs.
- Take out life assurance for the spouse who looks after the children. If he/she dies you will need to pay for childcare or work part time.
- Opt for a guaranteed premium. Some companies retain the right to 'review' (upwards) the premium whenever they want to.

Glossary of terms

Convertible renewable term assurance gives you the right to extend the insurance period without further medical underwriting, or in some cases to convert to an investment-linked plan.

Decreasing term assurance reduces at regular intervals, and can be used to protect a decreasing debt.

Family income benefit pays a regular income for the insured period.

Increasing term assurance automatically increases the level of cover – usually in line with retail price inflation or a fixed amount (say, 5 per cent) – without further medical underwriting.

Joint life covers two people, and can pay out either on the first death or only when the second person dies.

Level term assurance provides a tax-free lump sum if you die during the insured period.

Personal pension term assurance is available to the self-employed and employees not in company schemes.

Whole of life plans pay a benefit whenever you die and combine insurance with an investment plan.

Income protection insurance

Life assurance protects your family if you die, but it is equally important to insure against loss of income if you become disabled or too ill to work.

Disability or 'permanent health' insurance

This type of insurance goes under various names, for example disability insurance, income protection, or permanent health insurance (PHI). This is the unsung hero of a good employee benefits package. If your employer doesn't offer it – and only 11 per cent of UK workers are covered by a group PHI policy paid for by the company – then you should consider buying a private plan.

An increasing number of employers offer this type of benefit at a cheap rate even though they do not make a contribution towards your premiums. This type of voluntary benefit can offer excellent value but employers are under no obligation to arrange good terms, so *caveat emptor* – buyer beware – applies just as much if you buy through your employer as if you buy elsewhere. Insurance products sold through the workplace are discussed on page 163.

Your rights

Employees have very little statutory protection when it comes to long-term sickness. The only requirement for an employer is to pay statutory sick pay from day four of your illness to week 28. Statutory sick pay is about £65 per week, while the state long-term incapacity benefit is about £70, although there are various supplements for dependants. You can claim the state incapacity benefit while you are in receipt of your income replacement benefits.

The chances of qualifying for the state incapacity benefit are slim. In April 1995 the government changed the definition of qualifying disability from 'can't do *own* job' to 'can't do *any* job'. This means that even though your medical condition prevents you from continuing your profession, if you can sweep the streets you will be classed as fit for work and you will not qualify for the state long-term incapacity benefit.

PHI provides you with an income worth up to two-thirds of your salary and will maintain payments until you are well enough to return to work. To encourage you to return to work, where your employer pays the premiums you are unlikely to get the full salary replacement unless you are a very senior executive and your company is prepared to top up the insured benefit. If you are severely incapacitated, the replacement income should continue right up until your normal retirement date.

Your employer's scheme

Under a group PHI scheme the insurer pays the benefit to your employer who then deducts PAYE, National Insurance and pension contributions in the usual way before paying you. This means that you are able to remain an active member of your company pension scheme and maintain eligibility to state benefits.

PHI only replaces your income during the years you would actually have been at work. Once you reach your employer's normal retirement age the PHI benefit stops and your employer's pension scheme starts to pay you a retirement income.

Of course in most cases you would expect to return to work after a full recovery. At this point the benefit stops and your normal salary resumes. But what if you only partially recover from an accident or your recovery is not complete and you are unable to resume your former occupation? In these very common circumstances, assistance with rehabilitation forms an integral feature of top-of-the-range group PHI schemes.

> While critical illness insurance is a valuable benefit, it is not as comprehensive as PHI. If your illness or disability is not on the list of qualifying medical conditions, you will not receive any financial help.

It is important to find out how your company deals with long-term sickness. The company's policy should be set out in your contract of employment. For example, the contract might say that if you are ill the company will pay your full salary for a specified period, after which your pay will depend on the terms and conditions of the group PHI scheme.

Some of the larger employers self-insure absenteeism caused by long-term employee sickness. In this case they will set their own policy for continuing salary payments while you are off sick and if necessary may award you an ill health early retirement pension. The latter is paid out of the company's main pension scheme rather than through a separate insurance policy.

The majority of small to medium employers do not offer group PHI. Some provide group 'critical illness' insurance, which does not replace regular income but instead pays a tax-free lump sum on the diagnosis of major illnesses or accidents (see below).

While critical illness insurance is a valuable benefit, it is not as comprehensive as PHI. If your illness or disability is not on the list of qualifying medical conditions, you will not receive any financial help.

Individual policies

If your company does not offer income protection you should consider an individual policy. Only about 6 per cent of the population has this type of insurance, which according to the PHI specialist UNUM typically costs £350–400 per annum for a man in his mid-30s. Women pay much higher premiums due to the higher incidence of claims.

You can cut premiums if you opt for a long waiting period between the date you fall ill or become disabled and the date you claim benefit. The minimum waiting period is four weeks, but premiums reduce if you sign up for a three, six or twelve-month 'deferment' period. If you opt for a long deferment period, make sure you have enough savings to cover your outgoings while you are waiting for your income protection plan to kick in.

Advisers stress it is essential to link the insured income to retail price inflation, both during the insurance period and during the payment period. This will cost extra but without it the purchasing power of your income would quickly be eroded.

Watch out for PHI policies that have a 'reviewable' premium. This means you have no control over rate increases. You should also check the insurance company's definition of disability. This is the deciding factor when the company judges whether you are too ill to work and therefore are eligible to claim benefit. The best definition is 'unable to follow *own* occupation' with the possible addition of the phrase 'or an occupation

F I N A N C I A L   S N A P S H O T

Women typically pay 50 per cent more for income protection than men, due to the higher incidence of claims.

suitable by training, education, experience and status'. The worst definition, to avoid at all costs, is 'unable to follow *any* occupation'. Under the latter you have got to be totally incapacitated in order to claim – as is now the case with the state scheme.

Critical illness insurance

Critical illness insurance is often regarded as the poor man's PHI. However, this is a different type of insurance and if you can afford it you should have both. This type of insurance pays the owner of the policy – which could be you, your spouse or even your business partner – a tax-free lump sum on the diagnosis of a range of illnesses or accidents. Most policies use six standard definitions:

- cancer
- heart attack
- stroke
- coronary artery bypass surgery
- kidney failure
- major organ transplant.

If you are self-employed, the best way to protect your family should you become too ill to work is through a PHI policy. Critical illness lump sums are extremely helpful if you need to move to special accommodation or need to make alterations to your present home. However, unless your condition is on the list, you will not receive a penny even though you are unable to work. A good policy will include 'permanent total disability' on the payment list.

> Beware of vaguely worded exclusions relating to pre-existing conditions, as this type of clause can be interpreted very widely.

Critical illness insurance may create a potential inheritance tax bill. If you have a major illness before you die, your insurance lump sum will boost the value of your estate, and in the 2001–2002 tax year anything above £242,000 will be subject to IHT at 40 per cent. As mentioned, with term assurance you can avoid IHT by writing the policy in trust for your beneficiaries – your children or cat for example (yes, it does happen!). However, with critical illness you cannot do this if you yourself are the beneficiary.

Mortgage payment protection plans

There is nothing unique about mortgage protection plans – these are usually a combination of term assurance and a restricted version of PHI or critical illness insurance.

Term assurance is the simplest way to provide mortgage protection as this pays off the loan if you die. A special type of decreasing term assurance can be used where the debt reduces with time, as is the case with a repayment mortgage. For an interest-only loan, where the debt remains constant throughout the mortgage, you need level term assurance.

Where the policy you are offered includes an element of income protection, do check your existing cover first. If you take out more term assurance than you really need, at least your family will reap the benefits. However, if you over-insure with some of the income protection plans, you are not entitled to the excess, so some of your premiums will be wasted. As a rule, advisers reckon it is usually better to buy term assurance and critical illness or PHI separately to provide the right type and level of cover.

Another option you may be offered is **accident, sickness and unemployment (ASU)** insurance. This covers your monthly mortgage payments if you become too ill to work or are unemployed. The accident and sickness element is like a short-term PHI policy. Unemployment insurance is available through a few specialist companies but is very expensive, so ASU may be the only way to get it.

Following social security changes, if you are a new borrower and become unemployed, you now have to wait nine months before you can claim benefit to cover your mortgage – longer if you have savings of £8,000 or more. You can use ASU to insure the nine-month gap and in some cases can cover yourself for up to two years. However, experts warn that you should treat this type of insurance as a way of buying some breathing space if you need to re-assess your finances in the light of illness or unemployment. It does not provide a long-term replacement income.

Summary

- From April 1995 you can claim state incapacity benefit only if you are unable to do *any* job.
- Income protection or permanent health insurance plans can be used to replace up to two-thirds of your regular income.
- Specialist advice is essential – these policies are riddled with small print and vaguely worded clauses about pre-existing conditions.

- Make sure the premium rate is guaranteed not to rise, or is restricted to the rise in inflation. 'Reviewable' premiums can be increased at any time.
- The definition of eligibility for benefit should be 'unable to continue *own* job'.
- A good critical illness policy will include 'permanent total disability' on the eligible conditions list.

Glossary of terms

Accident, sickness and unemployment plans can be used to cover the nine-month period between loss of income and eligibility to claim the state benefit.

Critical illness policies pay the policy owner a lump sum on the diagnosis of one of a list of illnesses.

Income protection or **permanent health insurance** (PHI) pays a regular income, usually until you reach pension age.

Mortgage protection usually combines life assurance to repay the debt if you die and PHI to cover payments if you are too ill to work.

Long-term care

The problem of supporting a growing elderly population is not confined to the UK, although Germany is the only European country so far to introduce a tax specifically for nursing care. To date, the UK government has limited its consultation on long-term care (LTC) to voluntary insurance and savings plans. About 20,000 people have this type of insurance and most of these are in the 65–75 age range.

Under the NHS and Community Care Act 1993, the responsibility for assessing need and the payment of nursing home fees shifted from the Department of Social Security to the already financially overstretched local authorities. The rules are simple. If you have assets and investments worth over £16,000, you must pay your own bills, although under current proposals the NHS will pay the nursing care element, that is, about 25 per cent of the total bill. Of course in practice it is the residential care that is the most expensive long-term cost and this will remain your responsibility. Since your house is an asset, this is likely to be the first item to fall under the auctioneer's hammer unless you have a spouse or other dependent relative still living at home.

> At present, an estimated 40,000 homes are sold each year to pay for nursing home costs.

At present, an estimated 40,000 homes are sold each year to pay for nursing home costs. Once your house is sold, with typical nursing home fees of £15,000 to £20,000 per annum, depending on the area, it will not take long to spend your children's entire inheritance.

F I N A N C I A L   S N A P S H O T

Seven per cent of the over-75s live in care. The figure for the over-85s is nearer 30 per cent and growing. The number of people aged 75 and over will rise from 3.9 million now to 6.3 million by the year 2030.

Check your options carefully

If you are interested in LTC, seek the help of a specialist independent adviser. Most of these plans are complicated, expensive and they are not governed by the strict financial services regulatory system. One organization well worth contacting is IFACare, which is a voluntary association for independent advisers who agree to adhere to a high standard of ethics and a strict code of practice to ensure best advice is given on LTC. You should also seek legal advice. If you want to act on behalf of an elderly parent, for example, you must have enduring power of attorney in order to appoint a professional adviser to help manage your relative's affairs.

Before considering a dedicated LTC policy, check whether you are covered under other protection insurance plans. Some critical illness policies pay a cash lump sum if you suffer 'loss of independence'.

Finally, if you are tempted to give away all your worldly goods in order to qualify for full financial support under the social services means test, think twice. If you make a substantial gift within six months of entering care, your local authority may be able to claw back the assets. Where the gap is longer, the authority could take you to court.

WHAT THE STATE PROVIDES

■ If you have £16,000 or more in assets you will get no help towards nursing home fees. There is a sliding scale of benefits if you have between £10,000 and £16,000, and where your assets fall below £10,000 you qualify for the full assistance available, although this will vary from area to area.

Source: Department of Health

How to insure the cost of long-term care

There are two ways to insure the cost of long-term care. With a 'pre-funded' plan you pay regular premiums or a lump sum ahead of the time when you may need to claim. If you are elderly and not insured, an 'immediate care' plan would guarantee a regular income to pay the nursing home fees, but for this you would need to invest a substantial sum.

Pre-funding plans

At the time of writing, only half a dozen insurance companies offered pre-funding plans. The policies pay the benefit to your nursing home or, in some cases, to your carer. You may also qualify for help towards the cost of home alterations where this would enable you to stay put. Annual benefit, which is tax-free, usually is limited to about £25,000. However, most people can insure for much less than this if they have other sources of income from pensions and investments.

To qualify for benefit, you must fail two or three 'activities of daily living' (ADLs). ADL tests – also used by social services for those who qualify for state help – include washing, dressing, feeding, continence and mobility. Cognitive impairment should also be on the list, given the rapid increase in the number of sufferers of Alzheimer's disease and similar conditions.

As with income protection, you can reduce premiums if you opt for a long 'deferment period' before receiving the first payment. This can be anything from four weeks to two years. You can also reduce premiums if you restrict cover to a limited payment period, for example 2–3 years. However, whether you would enjoy peace of mind with this type of policy is questionable. Certainly, conditions that involve cognitive impairment can result in a lengthy stay in care.

The cost of insurance varies, but as a rough guide, a man aged 65 who wants to insure an annual benefit of £12,000 would pay monthly premiums of about £70 or a single premium of £9,500.

Immediate care annuities

If a relative needs to go into a home you might consider an immediate care annuity, although to fund this you may need to sell their house. Where the elderly person could stay at home, provided certain care was available and alterations were carried out, a home income plan might be more appropriate (see Chapter 17).

An annuity provides a regular income for life in return for your lump sum investment. One option for this age group is an 'impaired life annuity', as this offers a higher income if you have an illness which is likely to reduce your life expectancy.

The impairment must adversely affect life expectation and not just impact on the quality of life.

> If a relative needs to go into a home you might consider an immediate care annuity, although to fund this you may need to sell their house.

Qualifying impairments include AIDS, Alzheimer's, cancer, cirrhosis, coronary disease, diabetes and stroke. Depending on your impairment, you could secure an income up to 30 per cent higher than that offered by a standard plan. If you are interested, go to an annuity specialist who will select the best terms for your particular circumstances.

Unlike pre-funding plans, the annuity payments are not tax-free. Part of the income is treated as a return of capital so this is not taxed, but the interest element is taxed, although this reduces with age.

LTC investment alternatives

Long-term care is an insurance product, not an investment. Insurance relies on the pooling of risk, so the benefits of those who need to claim are paid for by the premiums of those who do not. This may be a price worth paying for peace of mind, but some investors regard it as money down the drain.

There is an alternative which combines investment and insurance, but it is relatively new and untested. Only a handful of companies offer this type of product. Under an LTC investment plan, you pay a lump sum into a fund from which the insurance company deducts monthly premiums to cover the LTC risk. The products currently available use funds which, for one reason or another, are able to offer gross roll-up (that is, the fund does not pay income and capital gains tax). This means that if your fund does well and the investment growth covers the cost of the monthly insurance, your LTC premiums effectively are tax-free.

If you need to claim, initially you draw your agreed annual benefit from your fund and when this is exhausted the insurer picks up the tab for as long as you remain in care. In some cases, for an extra cost, you may be able to protect part or all of your fund so that the insurance covers the benefit payments from the outset. However, if you remain healthy to the end and do not make a claim, you can pass your investment on to your dependants.

Summary

- Each year 200,000 people enter care.
- About 30 per cent of the over-85s live in nursing homes.
- Typically a resident can expect to pay between £15,000 and £20,000 a year in fees.
- If you have over £16,000 in assets, including the value of your house, you will get no help from the state.
- If you buy a long-term care policy, make sure it covers cognitive impairment.

- Only consider an investment-linked LTC product if you are happy with the level and cost of insurance and the risk level *and* performance of the fund.

Glossary of terms

Activities of daily living (ADLs) include washing, dressing, feeding, continence and mobility. To qualify for state help you must fail two or three of these tests.

Immediate care plans (annuities) guarantee a regular income for life in return for a lump sum investment.

Impaired life annuities offer a higher regular income because the insurance company assumes your life expectancy is less than that of a healthy person of your age.

Pre-funded long-term care policies require you to pay regular premiums or a lump sum ahead of the time when you might need to claim.

Further information

A list of independent firms of advisers which abide by the IFACare code of conduct is available from: Andrea Beech, IFACare Administration Office, Bridge House, Severn Bridge, Bewdley, Worcs DY12 1AB. Tel: 01299 406040. E-mail: *info@ifacare.co.uk*

Private medical insurance

The waiting list for many operations under the National Health Service is still well over a year, and that does not include the often lengthy period between GP referral and seeing a specialist. Regional variations in the provision of care can also make a huge difference to how quickly your particular condition will be treated.

If you want to jump the queue, you have to pay. While the more wealthy may decide to draw on cash reserves, for most people the only realistic option is to take out private medical insurance (PMI). About 11 per cent of the population have some form of private cover at a cost of more than £1.5 billion in annual premiums. Many employers offer group PMI, although this may only cover the employee and not his or her family. However, you may be able to buy family cover at preferential rates through your employer's 'voluntary benefits' scheme.

How it works

PMI is a complex product and contract conditions can be lengthy. With more than 25 companies each offering a range of options, it is wise to seek independent financial advice. An adviser should identify the best plan for your needs and price range and will know which insurers offer good service and are prompt with payments. Some advisers are able to offer better terms than are available if you buy direct from the PMI company.

It is important to understand exactly what conditions private medical insurance does and does *not* cover. PMI pays for private treatment for *acute curable conditions*, that is, cases where an operation

> Watch out for clauses that promise a 'full' refund and then qualify this statement in the small print by restricting payment to 'what is fair, reasonable and customary'. This can mean just about anything.

or a short-term course of treatment can put things right permanently. It does not pay for emergency treatment, or for treatments for chronic illness.

This can lead to confusion. For example, under your policy you may qualify for private treatment to have a condition investigated and diagnosed, but if it is a long-term illness rather than an acute curable condition, you could find yourself back on the NHS.

The premiums you pay for your PMI will depend on the level of cover you require, your age and your medical history. It will also depend on the type of hospital you choose to attend. Most insurers group hospitals into three bands – London teaching (the most expensive), national and provincial. Your adviser can help you choose the appropriate band for your area.

Different types of PMI

It is difficult to compare PMI policies because they all seem to offer something slightly different. However, most fall into three broad categories:

- standard
- budget
- over-60s.

Standard cover

Standard cover should pay for virtually everything, but if you want features such as private alternative medicine or private GP and dental treatment, you will probably have to pay for a deluxe version.

Budget plans

Budget plans limit the insurer's risk and your level of cover in several ways, so consider your priorities carefully. For example, a plan might restrict the

FINANCIAL SNAPSHOT

The provident associations, which dominate the PMI market, are being challenged by the heavyweight composite insurers such as CGNU and Legal & General. The biggest growth area is in 'budget' schemes that reduce premiums by restricting cover in some way.

treatment to a 'menu' of the most common operations. If your condition qualifies then you receive prompt treatment. If it doesn't, tough. A second method of reducing the insurers' costs is to set a monetary limit either per annum or per treatment. PMI companies claim these limits are usually generous enough to cover most major operations, but there is always the concern that you might run out of money halfway through a course of treatment, particularly if complications set in.

An alternative budget concept is the 'six-week' plan which provides standard levels of cover but only if you cannot be treated under the NHS within six weeks of the consultant's diagnosis. A six-week wait may not sound too onerous, but bear in mind that you may have a long delay between your GP's referral and actually seeing your consultant – unless of course you pay for a private consultation, which is unlikely to be covered by this type of policy.

Finally, some insurers contain costs by asking you to agree to pay an excess, that is, the first £100 or so of every claim. This is probably the most acceptable method of cutting premiums, although the reductions achieved are not as dramatic as under the other budget plans.

Over-60s plans

Over-60s plans cover the 60–75 age range and, until the Labour Budget of July 1997, offered basic rate tax relief on premiums. However, this was then abolished immediately for new policies and at the time of the annual renewal for existing policies.

Managed care

One of the latest trends in PMI is the use of managed care to contain costs. With managed care the insurer monitors the claim from the outset, before treatment has started and before the first penny has been spent. This means you have to check the insurer will pay up before you actually start treatment (this is known as 'pre-authorization'). You may also be asked to use certain groups of hospitals where the insurer has negotiated special rates.

Medical history

Unless you are in a top-of-the-range group scheme run by your employer, the PMI insurer will exclude most pre-existing conditions. This will be done in one of two ways. Where the contract is *fully underwritten*, you must disclose your complete medical history and the insurer may impose exclusions as a result. If there is a *moratorium clause*, you would not need to disclose your medical history but all pre-existing conditions would be excluded for a period of time – typically two years – after which they would also be covered. Some pre-existing conditions – heart disease and psychiatric illness, for example – may be permanently excluded.

Premium increases

When selecting your plan, your adviser should consider the PMI company's track record on premium increases. As with any form of general insurance, when your policy comes up for renewal each year, insurers can increase premiums without warning. Medical inflation tends to outstrip retail price inflation and typical rate increases in the late 1990s were more than 7 per cent. Increases were even higher in the early 1990s.

> As with any form of general insurance, when your policy comes up for renewal each year, insurers can increase premiums without warning.

If you are unhappy with the new premium, your only option is to vote with your feet and leave. However, if you already have a claim under way it may be impossible to switch insurers. It will also be awkward if you have made claims in the past five years since a new insurer would class any recent health problems as pre-existing conditions and exclude them. If your health has been particularly poor, you might even find yourself uninsurable.

Check your existing cover

As with any form of protection insurance, it is important to check existing cover before buying. There are two likely sources – the state and an employer's scheme.

What the state provides

The National Health Service aims to provide a full range of medical services for all residents regardless of their income. These services are financed mainly out of general taxation. Most forms of treatment, including hospital care, are provided free of charge 'at the point of delivery', to use the jargon. However, some treatment – eye tests, for example – must be paid for directly by the individual.

What your employer provides

Many employers offer group PMI as part of a benefits package, but the level of cover varies considerably and there is a general trend to reduce costs. Some group schemes have increased the number of exclusions, for example stress-related conditions are likely to be excluded since these can be complicated and expensive. Your employer may also ask you to pay an excess, or may agree to pay your premiums but will not cover your family. Premiums paid by your employer are treated as a benefit in kind and are therefore taxable.

An increasing number of employers offer PMI as a voluntary benefit. This means they do not pay for your premiums but instead use their bulk negotiating power to achieve competitive rates.

If you are in a group scheme, find out what happens when you leave the company if you want to continue the insurance on an individual basis. This is particularly important if you are coming up to retirement, when your age and past medical treatment could result in very high individual premiums. Some insurers offer a discount if you move from a group scheme to a private plan.

If your employer does not provide a scheme, check with your trade union or professional association to see whether they offer discount terms. Other organizations such as the AA and the RAC also offer affinity group discounts.

Summary

- PMI covers private treatment for *acute curable conditions* – cases where an operation or short-term treatment can put things right permanently.

- If you want to arrange private treatment, always check first with your insurer that your policy covers the treatment you need and at the hospital of your choice. Ask for written confirmation.

- Try to keep costs down and check your bill. Even though the insurance company is paying, if the hospital and consultant charges are excessive, eventually the cost will be passed on to policyholders through higher premiums.

■ If you are in your employer's scheme, check whether you can continue on an individual basis if you leave or retire.

Glossary of terms

Budget plans limit treatment by restricting cover to certain operations or by setting a monetary limit. Some budget plans offer private treatment only if you cannot be treated under the NHS within six weeks of diagnosis.

Managed care means that the insurer monitors costs throughout and pre-authorizes treatment.

Moratorium clauses exclude all pre-existing conditions typically for the first two years of the contract.

Over-60s plans are aimed at people aged between 60 and 75.

Standard PMI covers all mainstream treatment but may not cover alternative medicine and dental treatment. Some insurers offer deluxe plans which include these extras.

Taxation

Taxation and your investments

This book does not attempt to explain tax law and practice in great detail. Its main concern is with saving and investing wisely and, where applicable, making use of tax breaks to improve your returns. For this reason, most of the details on taxation are dealt with as they arise in the relevant chapters – on investments and protection insurances, for example.

Before you consider investing your spare capital, it is worth checking that you are making the most of your tax-free allowances and exemptions. This costs you nothing and can save you thousands of pounds. However, do not use your quota just for the sake of it. First look at how much tax you will save, and find out whether this is negated by complicated and expensive administration, as might be the case where you have to set up a trust.

> Do not use your tax allowances and exemptions just for the sake of it. First look at how much tax you will save and find out if this is negated by complicated and expensive administration.

Also, bear in mind that security and peace of mind are important. Gifts made to avoid tax must be outright, otherwise the Inland Revenue will see through the arrangement and continue to assess you on their value. Tax efficiency aside, you may rue the day you gave your favourite shares to your spouse or children.

Table 6.1 shows the main tax rates, allowances and exemptions. For more specific details, consult your accountant or the Inland Revenue. This chapter summarizes the most important allowances and exemptions which do not require expensive and complicated arrangements.

The personal allowances and exemptions for the 2001–2002 tax year, which apply to both spouses and children, are:

■ Income tax annual personal allowance – £4,535

■ Capital gains tax (CGT) annual exemption – £7,500

■ Inheritance tax annual exemption for gifts – £3,000.

Table 6.1 Main tax allowances and rates 2001–2002

Allowances/exemptions	
Personal allowance under 65	£4,535
Personal allowance 65–74	£5,990
Children's tax credit at 10%	£5,200
Annual CGT exemption	£7,500
Income tax	
Lower rate 10% on first	£1,880
Basic rate 22%[1] on next	£27,520
Higher rate 40% over	£29,400
Inheritance tax	
40%	over £242,000

[1] 20% on interest and dividends

Source: Inland Revenue

Income tax personal allowance

Your personal allowance is the amount you can receive before paying income tax. The source is irrelevant – it can be earned income or investment income. One of the best ways to save on income tax is to share income between spouses to make full use of the non-working or lower-earning spouse's allowance.

For example, transferring income from a higher-rate tax-paying spouse to a non-earning spouse can save over £1,500 in tax for the current year. If you also make use of the spouse's lower and basic rate allowance you can save over £6,000. You can achieve these savings either by giving your spouse income-producing assets or, if you run your own business, by paying your spouse a salary. If you opt for the latter method, make sure that you can justify the income to the Inland Revenue, and that you actually do pay it.

Don't forget that the allowance also applies to children. You could give your children income-producing assets, but you may need to set up a trust so that the income is not classed as your own. As a rule, if the annual income from your gift is more than £100, you, as parents, will be taxed on the lot. There are special trusts which avoid this, known as 'bare trusts', but check that the cost of setting up and running a trust is worth the tax saving. Remember, where the gift is from someone else – doting grandparents, for example – any income generated is classed as the children's and can be offset against the personal allowance.

F I N A N C I A L   S N A P S H O T

Since April 1990 married couples have been taxed separately. This means that both a husband and wife have a personal allowance for income tax and inheritance tax, as well as the annual exemption from capital gains tax.

Capital gains tax exemption

The exemption is the amount of post-inflation capital gains you can make in the current tax year before you pay CGT at your top rate of income tax. Gifts between spouses are exempt, so it makes sense to share assets in order to make use of both of your CGT exemptions.

Until the March 1998 Budget, the partner with a potentially high CGT bill could give shares to their spouse who could then bed and breakfast the shares – that is, sell them, realize the capital gains using the annual exemption and buy them back, usually the following day.

In the absence of B&B, wealthy investors should consult their accountant to discuss CGT mitigation arrangements. One option is to sell your shares and for your spouse to repurchase them – a process known as 'bed and spouse'. You incur a CGT liability when you make a 'chargeable gain' – that is, when you sell an asset and its value has increased since the time of purchase. The gain is the difference between the original purchase price and the sale price, allowing for an adjustment for inflation, known as the 'indexation allowance'.

This allowance applies up to April 1998, after which 'taper relief' kicks in, which reduces the rate of CGT according to how long you have held the asset.

Inheritance tax exemption

When you die, your estate will be liable to inheritance tax on anything over £242,000 (for the 2001–2002 tax year). Gifts between husbands and wives are exempt, but there are several other ways of making a cash gift without building up an IHT liability. Probably the most useful is the £3,000 annual gift which can be made by both spouses. You can increase this by a further £3,000 if you did not use last year's exemption.

In fact, there is nothing to stop you giving away any amount in excess of the exemption, but if you die within seven years, the tax assessment is based on when you made the gift and the date of death. A sliding scale operates, so the longer the period between the two dates, the lower the liability. This transaction, where you give assets to someone other than your spouse, is known as a 'potentially exempt transfer' and may be abolished in a future Budget.

> There is nothing to stop you giving away any amount in excess of the exemption, but if you die within seven years, the tax assessment is based on when you made the gift and the date of death.

If you and your spouse are likely to create a substantial IHT liability, you should discuss with your solicitor or accountant whether it is worth taking out a life assurance policy to cover the bill (see page 20). 'Joint life, second death, whole of life' policies written in trust are often used for this purpose. These combine insurance and investment. Your monthly premiums are invested, and from this fund the insurance company deducts the amounts necessary to provide the life cover. When you both die, the beneficiaries get the fund value or the sum assured, whichever is greater, free of tax. For potentially exempt transfers, where the potential liability decreases over the seven-year period after making the gift, you could use a decreasing term assurance policy to cover the bill. Remember, you only need to cover the potential tax liability, not the value of the entire gift.

There are several other useful IHT exemptions. For example, if your children get married you can give them each £5,000, while other relatives can give up to £2,500 free of any IHT liability. You can also make unlimited gifts to charities and political parties.

One further, under-used exemption is modest gifts from income. These are gifts that are normal or habitual and leave sufficient income for the donor to maintain his normal standard of living.

Summary

- Do not invest or set up complicated tax arrangements just for the tax benefits.
- The main tax allowances and exemptions you can take advantage of are income tax, capital gains tax and inheritance tax.

Glossary of terms

Bed and spouse: This is where you sell shares and your spouse repurchases them, usually the following day, to pocket the gain by making use of the CGT annual exemption.

Potentially exempt transfers are where you give assets to someone other than your spouse. If you survive for seven years there is no IHT to pay. Likely to be abolished in a future Budget.

Taper relief reduces the CGT rate for gains on assets held long term.

Making a will*

For most people, making a will is a simple and cheap exercise, and represents a small price to pay for your peace of mind and for the ease and comfort of your family. Yet only one in three adults bothers.

If you die without a valid will you die 'intestate'. If you have not yet made your will, remember the old saying, 'Where there's a will, there's a relative'. If you don't choose your beneficiaries, the government will do it for you.

This means the laws of intestacy will decide which of your dependants receive your money, while your friends and favourite charities will receive nothing. In particular, if you have young children, you will not have had the chance to make careful arrangements for their inheritance of capital (this would happen automatically at age 18 under the intestacy rules), and you will not have appointed the executors, the trustees and the children's guardians who will oversee their upbringing.

Remember also that there are certain events that render it essential to rewrite your will – in particular if you marry, divorce or remarry. As a general guide, even if there are no major changes relating to marriage or children, it is worth checking your will is up to date every five years.

Making a will does not involve a huge amount of work, unless your finances are very complicated. Most solicitors do the legwork for you, and simply ask you to complete a short form which provides the information they need to draw up a draft.

> Remember the old saying, 'Where there's a will, there's a relative'. If you want to choose the beneficiaries of your estate, you must make a will – otherwise the government will effectively choose for you.

* This chapter is based on Section 15 of *Kelly's Financial Planning for the Individual* by Simon Philip, published by Gee Publishing Ltd. Sections reproduced are by kind permission of the author.

Points to consider

When making a will, there are several common mistakes which can easily be avoided. For example, you should make sure you dispose of all of your estate, because if you do not, this could result in partial intestacy. You should also make provision for the fact that one of your main beneficiaries may die before you. Above all else, consider the legal rights of your dependants. If you do not make suitable provision, they may be unable to claim their right to a sensible provision under the law. Remember in this context that 'children' refers to legitimate, illegitimate and adopted children, although it does not usually include stepchildren.

You should also include any gifts to charities or specific gifts of assets to specific beneficiaries (for example your jewellery to your daughter/granddaughter). The trust powers of the trustees should also be set out here.

> Where you have young children, the appointment of willing and responsible guardians is essential, particularly where only one parent is alive.

Don't forget – you can use your will to make some important arrangements. For example, if you have a strong preference for burial or cremation, and know where you wish to be buried or your ashes to be scattered, this is the place to make your wishes known.

You should also discuss any specific role with an appointed executor or trustee before you put it in writing. These responsibilities can be onerous, or may conflict with some other role the individual already performs. Where you have young children, the appointment of willing and responsible guardians is essential, particularly where only one parent is alive.

Finally, if you own any property overseas, you should draw up a will under the terms of that country, taking care to ensure consistency with your UK will.

FINANCIAL SNAPSHOT

According to the Association of Solicitor Investment Managers (ASIM), two out of three people do not have a will, and as a result impose unnecessary administration and costs on their families and have no control over the choice of beneficiaries.

Executors and trustees

The executor is responsible for collecting your estate, and distributing it in accordance with the law. This can include paying any outstanding taxes and dealing with other financial affairs. The executor takes over from the date of your death, but is not officially appointed until the will is 'proved', and the appointment is confirmed by a grant of probate.

Most people appoint as an executor a spouse or close relative, plus a professional, for example your solicitor or accountant. Where the will includes a trust, it is helpful if the executor and the trustees are the same people.

What happens if you don't make a will

The main disadvantages of dying intestate are as follows:

- Your estate may not be distributed in accordance with your wishes.
- The appointed administrators may not be people whom you would have chosen – or even liked.
- It may take longer for the estate to be distributed, whereas when a will has been made an executor can take up his duties immediately after death.
- The costs may be greater, leaving less to pass on to your beneficiaries.
- Children will receive capital automatically at the age of 18, whereas you may have preferred this to take place later at a less 'giddy' age. What's more, the family home where your widow or widower lives may have to be sold to raise the capital.
- A testamentary guardian is not appointed for young children.
- Trusts may arise under an intestacy which produce complications, including statutory restrictions on the trustees' power to invest and advance capital.

Distribution of an estate under the laws of intestacy

The following details refer to the law in England and Wales. The laws that apply in Northern Ireland and in Scotland differ. 'Issue' refers to children (including illegitimate and adopted), grandchildren and so on. It does not include stepchildren.

If the deceased dies leaving:

- *A spouse but no issue, parent, brother, sister, nephew or niece:* The spouse takes everything.

- *A spouse and issue:* The spouse takes £125,000, personal 'chattels' (car, furniture, pictures, clothing, jewellery, etc) plus a life interest – that is the income only – in half of the residue. The children take half the residue on reaching age 18 or marrying before that age. In addition, on the death of the deceased's spouse, the children take the half residue in which the spouse had a lifetime interest.

- *A spouse, no issue, but parent(s), brother(s), sister(s), nephew(s) or niece(s):* The spouse takes £200,000, plus personal chattels, plus half the residue. The other half goes to whoever is living in order of preference: parents, but if none, brothers and sisters (nephews and nieces step into their parents' shoes if the parents are dead).

- *No spouse:* Everything goes to, in order (depending on who is still alive): issue, but if none, parents, but if none, brothers and sisters (nephews and nieces step into their parents' shoes). The pecking order then moves on to half-brothers and half-sisters or, failing them, their children, but if none, grandparents, but if none, uncles and aunts (cousins step into their parents' shoes), but if none, half-uncles and half-aunts (failing that, their children). If all of these relatives have died, the estate goes to the Crown.

Where part of the residuary estate includes a dwelling house in which the surviving spouse lived at the date of death, the spouse has the right to have the house as part of the absolute interest or towards the capital value of the life interest, where relevant.

Summary

- Only one in three adults in the UK has made a will.
- If you fail to make a will you will cause delays in the distribution of your estate and you have no control over the choice of beneficiaries.
- Use expert help when you draw up your will. A DIY will, unless very carefully worded, may prove invalid, in which case the laws of intestacy apply.
- Make sure all of the important details about your professional advisers and your financial affairs are set out for your executors.

Glossary of terms

Executors are the people who sort out your financial affairs after your death and are appointed in your will.

Guardians are appointed to help with the upbringing of your children.

Intestacy is where you die without a valid will. The laws of inheritance under intestacy are outlined above.

Issue refers to children (including illegitimate and adopted), grandchildren and so on. It does not include stepchildren.

Trustees are appointed to run any trusts you have, for example your children's inheritance which is held for them until they are 18 or older. Normally the trustees would be the same people as the executors.

Successful investment planning

The rules of the game

Many of the investments covered in this section are tax-efficient for at least one and sometimes several categories of investor.

If there is one piece of advice central to successful investing, it is this: never invest purely for the sake of obtaining tax relief. Your investments must be suited to your circumstances and must be able to stand up with or without the tax breaks.

So what criteria should you use in order to make the right choices? To answer this question, it is helpful first to go back to basics. In this chapter, we explain the relationship between risk and return and describe the most common asset classes. Your choice of assets – whether you hold them directly or through a collective fund – will be determined by your investment goals and your attitude to risk.

Risk

As an investor you will frequently come across the terms 'risk' and 'return'. Where an investment guarantees or aims to protect you from risk, you should be specific about the type of risk involved, and whether protection from one category exposes you to another. A good example is a building society deposit account. You can't get any safer than that. Or can you? The answer depends on which type of risk concerns you most. A deposit account with a major building society will protect you from capital loss, but

> As an investor you need to come to terms with that four-letter word 'risk'.

in real terms the interest rates offered rarely protect you from inflation. Your capital is 'safe', but it is exposed to inflation risk, so its real value – its spending power in today's terms – will be eroded over time by inflation.

Historically, if you wanted to match or beat inflation over the long term, you would have had to invest in equities. However, with equities, unless your fund provides a guarantee (and these inevitably lead to increased charges), your capital is at risk. Bonds – a type of IOU – offer the prospect of higher interest than a deposit account, but there is a risk that your capital may be eroded in order to provide you with a good regular income. Also, bonds generally pay a fixed rate of interest, so do not offer any protection against increases in inflation. This is also true of deposit accounts.

Return

Risk and return are inextricably linked. Any change to one will automatically affect the other. Essentially risk is the trade-off for return, or to put it another way, 'return' is the increase in value of your investment, and represents your reward for taking a risk. If the risk pays off, your return could be substantial, but the reverse is also true. And clearly, the greater the level of risk, the greater the potential reward or loss. So, if you invest all your money in a single company's shares and it does well, you will be in clover. If the company goes bust, you could lose everything.

You can spread risk through collective funds such as unit and investment trusts, and open-ended investment companies, or through insurance company funds. But even here the risk rating ranges from higher-risk small specialist funds to large international funds which offer greater immunity to the capricious behaviour of particular markets and shares. Bear in mind, however, that even the most broadly diversified funds will be hit when stock markets crash.

Asset classes

Savings and investment institutions are adept at dressing up what are essentially quite straightforward assets which can be used to meet certain needs. For example, if you are saving for the short term and need a steady and secure income, the assets most likely to match this requirement are

FINANCIAL SNAPSHOT

Equities are considered more risky and volatile than bonds because they behave in an unpredictable way, whereas, provided the company or government backing a bond is secure, the return on a bond held to maturity is predictable.

fixed-interest securities, bonds and cash – all of which are low-risk investments that generate a stream of income. If, however, you are saving over 25–30 years for your pension or to build up a fund to repay your mortgage, you should consider taking greater medium-term risks in return for potentially higher rewards. In this case you are more likely to invest in equities.

Stocks and shares

Investment literature is often confusing, so it helps to understand the jargon. Commonly used (and misused) terms include 'securities', 'stocks' and 'shares'. 'Securities' is the general name for all stocks and shares. Broadly speaking, stocks are fixed-interest securities and shares are the rest. The four main types of securities listed and traded on the London Stock Exchange are:

- UK ('domestic') equities – ordinary shares issued by UK companies
- Overseas equities – ordinary shares issued by non-UK companies
- UK gilts – bonds issued by the UK government to raise money to fund any shortfall in public expenditure
- Bonds or fixed-interest stocks – issued by companies and local authorities, among others.

The following guide may help the uninitiated.

UK equities

UK equities are the quoted shares of companies in the UK and tend to dominate most private investors' portfolios, whether the investments are held directly or are pooled. Companies 'go public' by being quoted on the Stock Exchange or Alternative Investment Market in order to raise finance by issuing shares. A share literally entitles the owner to a specified share in the profits of the company and, if the company is wound up, to a specified share of its assets.

> The 'dividend yield' on equities is the dividend paid by a company divided by that company's share price. This is an important feature for income seekers.

The owner of shares is entitled to the dividends – the annual or six-monthly distribution to shareholders of part of the company's profits. The 'dividend yield' on equities is the dividend paid by a company divided by that company's share price. This is an important feature for income seekers.

There is no set redemption date for an equity: if the holder wishes to realize its value he must sell it through a broker. The price will vary from day to day, so the timing of the purchase and selling of shares is critical.

There are different classes of shares. 'Ordinary' shares give the holder a right to vote on the constitution of the board of directors. 'Preference' shares carry no voting rights but have a fixed-dividend payment and have preference over ordinary shareholders if the company is wound up.

The return achieved by UK equities, when measured over the long term, has exceeded both price and earnings inflation.

There are several sub-classes of equities or equity-related investments.

Convertibles and warrants   Convertibles (also known as convertible loan stocks or convertible bonds) confer a right to convert to an ordinary share or preference share at a future date. You might also come across warrants, which confer a right but not an obligation on the holder to convert to a specific share at a pre-determined price and date. The value of the warrant, which itself is traded on the stock market, is determined by the difference or premium of the share price over the conversion price of the warrant.

Derivatives   Derivatives, as the name suggests, derive their value from the price of an underlying security. This is the generic term given to futures contracts and options, both of which can be used to hedge risk in a fund or even in a large private portfolio.

A futures contract binds two parties in a sale or purchase at a specified future date at a price that is fixed at the time the contract is taken out. These can be used by institutional funds to control risk by quickly increasing or reducing exposure to an existing asset class. Futures have also proved popular as a cost-cutting mechanism, particularly in index-tracking funds and other funds where there are rapid changes of large asset allocations.

Options are more speculative financial instruments, whereby the payment of a sum of money confers the right but not the obligation to buy or sell something at an agreed price on or before a specified date.

Derivatives can be extremely risky, and great care should be taken to check that an investment manager is following prescribed guidelines. In general, it is considered less risky if derivatives are used for hedging and similar risk management techniques rather than speculation, but in some cases this may be a difficult line to draw. Also, guarantees do not come free, and if derivatives are used for this purpose, you will pay more for the investment management as a result.

Overseas equities

These are similar in principle to UK equities, but there are differences in shareholder rights. Investment overseas offers the opportunity to gain exposure to foreign currency and younger, fast-growing economies, but there can be tax penalties on the investments, because some or all of the withholding tax on dividends deducted by the foreign country may not be recoverable. Moreover, in the case of developing markets, there may be a risk of sequestration.

Bonds

Bonds behave like a sophisticated IOU. UK bonds are issued by borrowers, for example the government (these bonds are known as 'gilt-edged securities' or just 'gilts') and companies (corporate bonds). Bonds are also issued by local authorities, overseas governments and overseas companies.

In return for the loan of your money, the borrower agrees to pay a fixed rate of interest for the agreed period, and to repay your original capital sum on a specified date, known as the maturity date.

UK domestic bonds are either secured on the company's underlying assets – for example the company's property – or they are unsecured, in which case there is no physical asset backing the bond's guarantee to pay interest, and to repay the capital at maturity. Secured bonds are known as debentures, and unsecured bonds are known as loan stocks. Since the security offered by debentures is greater than for loan stocks, the former tend to pay a lower rate of interest.

The point to remember about fixed-interest securities is that the investment return is determined more by the level of interest rate than the issuing company's profitability. Provided the issuer remains sufficiently secure to honour the future coupon payments (the regular interest) and redemption payment (the return of the original capital), you know exactly what your return will be if you hold the bond to maturity. Gilts offer the highest degree of security because they are issued by the UK government.

If the fund manager sells a bond before its maturity date, the value of the future coupon and redemption payments will depend on the prevailing interest rates at the time of sale. If interest rates are high, then the value of the fixed-interest security will be lower because you could get a similar return for less money elsewhere. Conversely, if interest rates are low, then the value of the fixed-interest security will be higher because it provides a greater stream of income than you could get from alternative sources. This volatile pattern of behaviour is more apparent with fixed-interest securities which have a long period to run to maturity, since they are more likely to be traded before redemption date.

Index-linked gilts

Index-linked gilts are issued by the UK government and are guaranteed to provide interest payments and redemption proceeds which increase in line with inflation. For this reason they are one of the lowest risk assets for

64

PERSONAL FINANCIAL PLANNER

income seekers. The return on index-linked gilts in excess of the retail price index varies, but usually it is possible to buy these securities in the market-place at a price which guarantees a real rate of return to the holder, assuming that the stock is held to maturity.

Cash

Cash does not refer to stacks of £10 notes stuffed under the mattress. Institutional investment in cash is very similar to an individual's investment in a building society or bank deposit account. Deposits have the advantage that the value in monetary terms is known and is certain at all times. What is unknown is the interest that will be received.

> Cash does not refer to stacks of £10 notes stuffed under the mattress.

Property

In investment terms, 'property' usually refers to the ownership of land and buildings that are used by a business or other organization. The owner receives income from rent charged to the tenant and, over time, this rent is expected broadly to keep pace with inflation. The dominant factor in the value of a property is the desirability or otherwise of its position.

There are several problems with property. First, it is often sold in large blocks which cannot be easily split for investment purposes. As a result, only the larger institutional funds can afford to own property directly. Second, property is a very illiquid asset and it can take several years for the right selling conditions to arise. Also, unless you invest via a collective fund, you cannot dispose of your investment piecemeal to make best use of your annual capital gains tax exemption, but instead could be landed with a whopping CGT bill on your profits.

Comparing equities, bonds and cash (deposits)

It is common practice to compare returns on equities and bonds with cash (deposits). Generally, when inflation is taken into account deposits do not keep pace with inflation. If you put your money in a deposit account, it will increase with the interest earned, but over the long term the value of its real spending power will fall.

Barclays Capital has published an annual Equity-Gilt Study since 1956, which compares short, medium and long-term returns from equities, gilts and cash. Historically the overriding message has been that over the long term the equity investor is rewarded for taking risk because the degree of payoff – in the form of enhanced return – has been substantial relative to gilts and cash.

The volatility of equity markets during the 1990s, and the comparatively good performance of bonds and gilts, has changed that view. Barclays Capital said: 'The received wisdom that long-term investors should concentrate their assets in the equity market is an oversimplification. The case for equity investment may be weak if an investor can realize his or her objectives by means of a less risky strategy.'

Period of investment

Clearly, long-term returns on equities, gilts and cash should be viewed with some caution and certainly should not be treated as a guide to the future. While it seems likely that equities will provide a better return than bonds over the medium to long term, there is an important caveat. 'Medium to long term' means a minimum of five years, preferably longer. If you go into the stock market for shorter periods, you are in danger of getting your fingers burned, either because the markets take a tumble just before you want to get out, or because the fixed costs associated with setting up your investment undermine the return in the short term.

Stock selection

Stock selection refers to the process where the investment manager chooses individual securities. The following paragraphs over-simplify the process but nevertheless may help explain the jargon that investment managers love to use to confuse.

One important point to remember is that large institutional funds can make money on minor price changes because of the sheer volume of their transactions. Moreover, compared with a private client, many institutional funds – the big pension and charity funds, for example – also benefit from very low dealing costs and automatic exemption from among other things capital gains tax.

Active managers

Active investment managers aim to add value by deviating from a specific benchmark, for example a stock market index. There are two basic techniques used in active stock selection.

The starting point for active managers who adopt a **bottom-up** approach is the company in which the manager is considering making an investment. The manager will look at in-house and external research on the company's history and potential prospects. This will include an examination of the strength of the balance sheet, the company's trading history, the management's business strategy and the price/earnings ratio (the market price of a share divided by the company's earnings/profits per share in its latest 12-month trading period). From the company analysis, the manager will proceed to look at the general performance and prospects for that sector (oil, transport and so on) and then take into consideration national and international economic factors.

The **top-down** manager works in reverse, looking first at the international and national economic factors that might affect economic growth in a country or area such as emerging markets or a sector such as technology, and gradually working down to the individual companies.

Passive managers

Passive managers aim to track or replicate a benchmark. This style is also known as index tracking. It may sound simple, but in practice this is a complex process based on emulating the performance of a particular stock market index by buying all or a wide sample of the constituent shares, using a computer model to achieve this. The passive manager does not consider the merits of each stock, of different sectors and economic cycles. If it is in the index then it must be represented in the fund. Where the process tries to outstrip the index returns by deviating in a specific way, it is known as quantitative management.

> Passive managers aim to track or replicate a benchmark. This style is also known as index tracking.

Comparing different investments

Before you consider the various investment options outlined in the following chapters, get acquainted with the benchmarks set out below. It doesn't matter if you are looking at plain-vanilla deposit accounts or high-risk arrangements such as enterprise investment schemes, which invest in the shares of unquoted trading companies – the benchmarks will help you judge them all. They will also help you to focus on the important fundamentals as opposed to the bells and whistles that are used in marketing literature to make products look clever.

- **Aims:** What are the stated aims, benefits and possible uses of the investment?

- **Returns:** Compare the potential net returns with after-tax returns on very low-risk investments such as 120-day-notice building society deposit accounts, short-term conventional gilts and National Savings. Is the potential outperformance of your chosen investment really worth the additional risk?

- **Alternatives:** Which other investments share similar characteristics? Are they simpler/cheaper?

- **Direct investment or collective funds?** Everyone's financial circumstances and requirements are different, but as a rough guide experts suggest that for those with £100,000 or more to invest (some put the figure as high as £200,000) it may be cost effective to build a direct equity and bond portfolio, using collective funds to gain access to specialist sectors and overseas markets. For investors with less than £100,000 it makes sense to use collective funds for the main core holdings where economies of scale reduce dealing and administration costs, and the spread of investments within the fund reduces risk and provides better access to overseas markets.

- **Investment period:** Never mind the flannel, for how long is your money really tied up? Check how the charges undermine returns in the early years and make sure you know about any early exit penalties.

- **Risk:** What is the most you can lose if you stay the course or pull out early? Check how risk affects your capital and income and look at the likely effect of inflation. Find out how the investment is regulated and what happens if the firm/investment manager goes bust.

- **Cost:** Look at the establishment costs and ongoing charges. Watch out for high annual management charges, particularly for long-term investments, as these will seriously undermine your return.

- **Tax:** The way the fund and you, the investor, are taxed is important because it will reduce your ultimate return. Check for income and capital gains tax implications.

The FTSE indices

The total market capitalization of the FTSE (Financial Times Stock Exchange) monitored indices – that is all 1,500 or so stocks in the UK – was £1,797bn at the end of 2000.

With the exception of the Fledgling, all the indices are reviewed every quarter (March, June, September and December). The Fledgling is reviewed annually in December.

The FTSE indices are arithmetically weighted by market capitalization so that the larger the company, the greater the effect its share price movement will have on the relevant index. Market capitalization is the stock market valuation of the company. This is calculated by multiplying the number of shares in issue by their market price.

The UK indices in which you will invest directly or through collective funds are as follows:

■ **The FTSE All-Share** is the most comprehensive index. This consists of just over 770 companies with a total market capitalization of about £1,720bn. The All-Share is regarded as the professional investor's yardstick for the level of the UK equity market as a whole and represents about 98 per cent of UK stock market capitalization. Within the All-Share companies are allocated to 39 industrial sectors.

■ **The FTSE 100 index** consists of the 100 largest companies by market capitalization. Together they represent about 78 per cent of the total UK stock market capitalization (not just the All-Share).

■ **The FTSE 250 index** consists of the next 250 companies below the FTSE 100 and can include or exclude investment trusts. There are no fixed parameters for market capitalization but the companies currently in this index are capitalized at between £350m and £3bn. Together these 250 companies represent about 13 per cent of the UK stock market capitalization (including investment trusts).

■ **The FTSE SmallCap index** does not have a fixed number of constituent companies as it comprises all the remaining companies in the All-Share that are too small to qualify for the top 350. Together they account for about 4.4 per cent of the total market capitalization.

■ **The Fledgling** index covers about 680 companies that are too small for the All-Share. Together the SmallCap and Fledgling are known as the All-Small index.

■ **Alternative Investments Market**, or Aim, is the market for young and growing companies, which are likely to be higher risk than companies admitted to the London Stock Exchange's Official List. There are just over 500 companies in Aim.

Summary

- Building society deposit accounts have their place as a home for an emergency fund and short-term cash, but interest rates are unlikely to match inflation over the long term, especially for taxpayers.

- Your choice of investment will be determined by how much risk you can afford to take to boost your chances of an enhanced return.

- Historical data show that over the long term, equities outperformed bonds and deposit accounts, but this was not the case during the 1990s.

- You can spread risk through collective funds but you must still consider asset allocation and your exposure to risk and examine how well a fund or your total portfolio is diversified.

- Use the benchmarks provided to compare the most important features of different types of investment.

Glossary of terms

Active managers aim to beat a stock market index through research into companies and markets.

Bonds are IOUs issued by governments and companies, among others. In return for your loan of money, the borrower pays you a fixed rate of interest while the loan is outstanding and, at a specific date in the future repays the capital. Bonds can be **secured** – for example on the company's property – or **unsecured**.

Convertibles confer a right to convert to an ordinary share or preference share at a future date.

Collective funds spread risk because they invest in many different equities and/or bonds and/or other securities. Your money buys you units (in the case of unit trusts) or shares (in the case of investment trusts) in the fund.

Derivatives literally 'derive' their value from the price of an underlying equity. This is the generic term used to describe futures contracts and options, both of which can be used to hedge risk.

Dividends are the annual or six-monthly distribution to shareholders of part of the company's profits.

Equities are the ordinary share capital of a company. In return for your investment, you receive a share in the company's profits.

Gilts are bonds issued by the UK government.

Passive managers aim to keep returns in line with an index performance by replicating some or all of the index companies.

Securities is the general name for stocks (fixed interest) and shares (equities).

Stock picking: *Bottom-up stock picking* means your investment manager will analyze company details first, then consider the results in the context of the prospects for that sector and in the context of national and international economic forecasts. *Top-down stock picking* is the reverse, where the manager will start with international factors, proceed to country forecasts, economic forecasts, and then focus on the prospects for a particular sector. Individual stock picking is the final stage in the top-down process.

Warrants confer a right but not an obligation on the holder to convert to a specific share at a pre-determined price and date.

Further information

Barclays Capital Equity-Gilt Study 2001. ***www.barclaysglobal.com***

Buying, selling and monitoring your investments

This chapter explains how to buy, sell and monitor some of the most popular types of investments. Savings which offer a fixed or variable rate of interest – deposit accounts, National Savings, gilts and bonds, among others – are examined in Chapter 10.

Most investment managers would argue, quite rightly, that good performance more than outweighs a high initial or annual management charge. However, since it is impossible to predict performance it makes sense to ensure that returns are not undermined by excessive costs. This is particularly important at present as we seem to have entered a prolonged period of low interest rates, low inflation and comparatively low investment returns.

Be particularly careful when you are looking at the so-called 'tax efficient' investments. Your best approach is to ignore the hype and consider instead a simple question: Do the charges outweigh the tax advantages? This is especially important for those investing smaller sums and for basic and lower rate taxpayers where the charges may be disproportionately high compared with the tax benefits.

> Your best approach is to ignore the hype and consider instead a simple question: Do the charges outweigh the tax advantages?

It is a regulatory requirement for investment companies to provide investors with a pre-sale 'key features' document which sets out the charges and how they build up over different investment periods. This will help you make comparisons between different managers who offer essentially the same product, and also between entirely different investments.

The following section looks at the charges for one of the most popular investments – unit trusts individual savings accounts.

The charges

The initial charge

The initial charge is deducted immediately from the original capital invested. It is calculated as a percentage of the lump sum – typically 5 per cent on a UK unit trust, although this is often discounted, particularly if you buy online. The charge may include your adviser's sales commission, if applicable, which is likely to account for about 3 per cent.

An increasing number of the low-cost Isas – the index-tracking funds for example – keep their charges to a minimum by eliminating the middle man and selling direct to the public. In this case there may not be an initial charge at all. Many discount brokers also reduce or eliminate this charge. However, as discussed below, the annual charge is probably the most important figure you should look at.

The bid/offer spread

The initial charge does not reveal the full upfront costs, which instead are shown in the bid/offer spread (the difference between the buying and selling price). This is likely to be 0.5 per cent higher than the initial charge and in some cases the increase may be as much as 3 per cent.

The bid price is the price at which the manager will buy back the units, and therefore the price at which the investor sells. The offer price is the price at which the manager sells units, and therefore the price at which the investor buys. The 'spread' includes stamp duty, among other items, and as such represents the true purchase cost of the investment.

The annual management charge

This represents the cost of the investment management and administration and is deducted as an annual percentage of the fund, so its value grows along with your fund. The annual charge also includes the cost of any 'trailer' or 'renewal' commission paid to financial advisers. This is the annual commission that is paid from year two onwards – typically 0.5 per cent of your fund value.

Initial vs annual

Although the initial charge often appears the most significant deduction, advisers warn that it is the compound effect of high annual charges that most damage your prospects of a good return over the long term.

For this reason you should watch out for unit trust Isa companies which have lowered or abolished their initial charges (often compensated by equally high 'exit' charges if you pull out early) and raised their annual charge. A typical exit penalty might be 4.5 per cent of your fund in year one, 4 per cent in year two, 3 per cent in year three, 2 per cent in year four and 1 per cent in year five.

Isa wrapper charges

Unit trust managers may add an extra layer of cost on top of the charges for the underlying unit trust to cover Isa administration but this is unusual. In practice most managers charge the same whether or not you invest through an Isa wrapper.

How to get the best deal

Unless you are an experienced investor you probably should seek help from an independent financial adviser and accept you will have to pay for the advice. However, there are opportunities for investors who know what they want and are looking for the cheapest way to buy. In particular the Internet offers a huge range of funds, usually at a discount. You can also buy a range of funds with your annual Isa allowance through 'fund super-markets'. These are discussed below.

Buying and selling

Shares

How you buy your shares (this includes investment trust shares) will depend on the nature of the agreement you have with your stockbroker or investment manager. If you have a discretionary or advisory manager, the firm will act on your behalf once you have completed a terms-of-business agreement and paid a cash and/or stock deposit. The firm will provide a tariff of charges automatically.

If you don't already have a stockbroker, the best source is the Association of Private Clients and Investment Managers (Apcims) directory (*www.apcims.co.uk*). This explains the different types of stockbroker agreements and provides websites for member firms, including those that offer an execution-only service on the Net.

Collective funds

Buying units in a unit trust, an open-ended investment company or unit linked insurance company funds should be straightforward. The confident investor can buy directly off the individual company websites and also from fund supermarkets, which allow you to buy from a range of providers within your annual Isa allowance. The personal finance pages of the national press cover fund supermarkets on a regular basis, but a couple worth looking at are **www.egg.com** and **www.fidelity.co.uk.**

Within a few days of sending off your application or placing your order by phone you will receive a contract note which will confirm your investment, giving details such as the price, type and number of units.

Assuming you are satisfied that the timing is appropriate, it is easy and quick to sell unit trusts. You can either sell your total holding or just some of your units, provided you leave in sufficient to meet the manager's minimum investment requirements.

> Once the manager receives your instruction you should get your cheque, accompanied by a 'sell' contract note, within a week.

The documents you receive when you make your investment and the regular manager's reports should include an explanation of how to sell units. This may involve completing a special withdrawal form on the back of your unit trust certificate or it may be sufficient to send a written instruction. Alternatively you could ask your adviser to arrange a withdrawal for you.

Once the manager receives your instruction you should get your cheque, accompanied by a 'sell' contract note, within a week.

Income payments

If you elect to receive income you will do so on fixed dates each year, half year or at whatever frequency you have agreed. Income is usually paid directly into your bank account unless you ask for it to be reinvested.

Monitoring performance

For shares, the *Financial Times* is the best source of information. The *FT* also covers collective funds but there are several additional sources of reference, for example the useful articles, surveys and statistics which appear in financial publications such as *Investors Chronicle*, *Money Management*, *Bloomberg Money* and *Moneywise*, all of which are available from newsagents.

KEEP TRACK OF YOUR UNIT PRICE USING THE FT AUTHORISED UNIT TRUST SERVICE

Name of the investment group, its pricing system and trust names: This is shown as, for example, 'ABN AMRO Fund Managers (0800)F' followed by the company's address and telephone number for dealing or enquiries. Use this number if you want to get a free copy of the management group's most recent report and scheme particulars. Under each company are listed its authorised unit trusts and open-ended investment companies.

The figure in brackets in the heading is the basis of the company's pricing system. This refers to the time at which the price was measured (using a 24-hour clock) and the basis of calculation. 'F' means forward pricing, where orders are taken from investors and the price of units is determined by the next valuation. All larger groups have a valuation point each day, often at noon. So, if you phone your order at 10am, the price will be struck at noon that same day. An investor who phones at 1pm will have to wait for a price until the following midday valuation.

Some groups still deal on an historic price basis, indicated by 'H'. This means they buy and sell using the price agreed at the last valuation point.

Initial charge (Init chrge): The second column shows the percentage charge deducted from your investment to cover certain costs – for example administration and the sales commission paid to advisers, if applicable. If the charge is 5 per cent, then £95 out of every £100 will actually be invested in your chosen fund.

Notes: The third column lists symbols and letters which represent particular features. For example, 'E' indicates there is an exit charge when you sell your units, 'C' indicates that the manager's annual charge is deducted from capital, not income. A full list of notes can be found at the end of the 'FT Managed Funds' section.

Selling price: This is also known as the 'bid price' – the price at which investors sell units back to the manager.

Buying price: This is also known as the 'offer price' – the price at which investors buy units.

Price change (+ or -): The sixth column compares the mid-point between the bid and offer prices with the previous day's quotation.

Yield: This column shows the income paid by the unit trust as a percentage of the offer price. Bond funds tend to quote the gross redemption yield after charges but before tax. Equity funds usually quote a yield that represents the estimated annual payout net of tax for basic rate taxpayers.

For more frequent updates you can check the price in the authorized unit trusts pages in the *Financial Times* (see Figure 9.1). On Saturdays the information appears in the 'Weekend Money' section, while on weekdays you will find these figures in the 'Companies and Markets' section. Compare percentage price changes with changes in an appropriate benchmark, for example the FTSE All-Share (see page 68).

Figure 9.1 Authorized investment funds

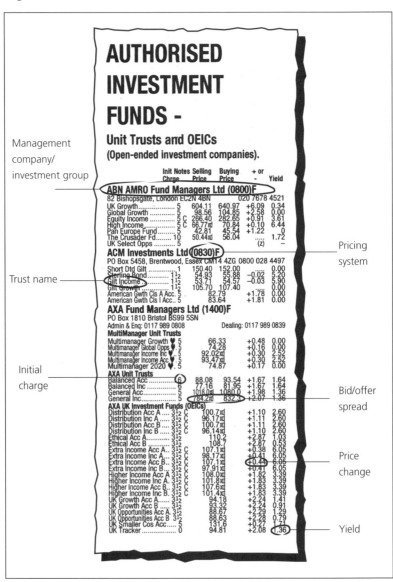

If you find reading the pink pages rather daunting, a basic description of the column headings is provided in the *FT* itself. A more detailed source is *The Financial Times Guide to Using the Financial Pages* (see Further information below).

Periods of measurement

The costs of buying shares, whether direct or through a unit or investment trust, combined with the short-term volatility of markets, has meant that performance tends to be measured over the medium to long term – typically over a minimum period of five years. While this is a sensible approach for private investors, it should be backed up by more regular monitoring which will pick up on changes in fund management style or personnel.

Summary

- The annual charge is the one to watch on medium to long-term investments.
- If your adviser gives up some or all of the initial commission, find out if he is receiving trailer commission instead.
- Your adviser or plan manager must disclose the full cost of your investment in a pre-sale 'key features' document.
- For Isa investments, find out exactly what information you will receive – for example if you want to see the company or trust's annual report and accounts, do you have to pay extra?
- Be prompt when your adviser asks for the money/shares and other paperwork necessary to settle a deal.
- Nominee accounts can help speed up settlement, but do check that your adviser accepts responsibility for any losses made by the nominee company.

Glossary of terms

Accumulation units: If you buy this type of unit in a unit trust, the income generated remains within the fund.

Advisory management is where you and your manager discuss investment decisions and the manager cannot act without your prior approval.

Annual management charge: This is the percentage of your fund which is deducted by the financial institution to cover investment management and administration.

Bid/offer spread: The difference between the price at which you buy (offer price) and sell (bid price) your units. This includes additional items such as stamp duty, which are not included in the initial charge so the 'spread' shows the full cost of your plan.

Discretionary management is where your plan manager makes all the investment decisions for you.

Execution only is where you make all the investment decisions and your stockbroker simply buys and sells on your instructions. No advice is provided.

Exit charges: Additional charges imposed as a penalty if you pull out early.

Income units: If you hold these units in a unit trust, any income generated by the trust's investments will be paid to you on set dates.

Initial charge: The cost of buying your Isa, including sales commission to your adviser, if applicable.

Further information

The Stock Exchange publishes useful leaflets on buying and selling shares and on rolling settlement and nominee accounts. For copies, telephone 0207 797 1000 or write to the Stock Exchange, London EC2N 1HP (**www.londonstockexchange.com**).

For a list of contacts, see Appendix 2.

The Financial Times Guide to Using the Financial Pages, by Romesh Vaitilingam, published by FT Prentice Hall. Contact the Professional Marketing Department, Pearson Education Ltd., 128 Long Acre, London WC2E 9AN. Tel: 020 7379 7383.

Lower-risk savings and investments

'Safe', like 'risk', means different things to different people. It might be 'safe' to shift your pension fund into long-dated gilts and deposits in the run-up to retirement, but it would be far from prudent to adopt the same investment strategy for a personal pension in your early thirties. The phrase 'reckless conservatism' aptly sums up the hidden risks in going for investments which appear to be safe but in fact are wholly inappropriate and therefore expose you to the risk that inflation will seriously damage your long-term returns.

> The phrase 'reckless conservatism' aptly sums up the hidden risks in going for investments which appear to be safe but in fact are wholly inappropriate.

This chapter, which is aimed primarily at those with short-term savings needs and investors looking for income, takes you through the various savings and investment opportunities where important guarantees are offered – but at a price. The trick is to recognize the guarantees for what they are, use them wisely, but avoid the trap of investing too much in products that are not designed to provide capital growth.

Before you invest any money it is important to be sure it really is surplus. If you have checked you have the essential protection insurance for you and your family (see Section 2), then it is time to consider your slush fund.

Easy-access deposits for rainy days

All investors need an immediate access emergency fund to pay for unforeseen events such as sudden repairs on the house and car. However, this is not a role for equity-based investments. If you have to pull out of an equity unit trust in a hurry you could lose money, particularly in the early years when your investment is 'working off' the effect of initial charges or when the investment manager may impose an exit charge. You also need to time sales of equities carefully due to the volatility of markets.

The traditional home for cash is the building society. Stick with it, but avoid the common mistake of keeping too large a reserve when part of your money could be earning a potentially better return elsewhere.

The size of your emergency fund should be determined by your monthly expenditure, your liabilities and the level of padding you feel is appropriate for your lifestyle and peace of mind. As a very rough guide it is worth keeping three times your monthly outgoings in an account that has one week's notice. Accounts offering a higher rate of interest with, say, three months' notice can be used for known future capital expenditure – for example a new car, a holiday or school fees. If you manage your cash flow carefully then you can feed money from your other investments to your high-interest-rate account well in advance of the dates these more substantial bills fall due. But keep a regular check on your longer-term deposits as rates change frequently. Postal and Internet accounts tend to offer the best rates.

Probably the best source of up-to-date information on savings products is the monthly *Moneyfacts* guide to mortgage and savings rates, which covers everything including savings accounts, children's accounts, cheque accounts, credit cards, store cards, bonds, gilts, mortgages, National Savings, and loans. *Moneyfacts* also publishes a separate monthly guide to life assurance and pension products. Subscription details are provided at the end of this chapter.

You can find useful information on the best rates for a variety of savings accounts in the personal finance pages of the weekend newspapers. Most papers publish useful summaries of best buys for different types of products and accounts (many of which are provided by *Moneyfacts*).

Safety at a price

Before you lock in to a fixed-income product remember that if interest rates rise you will have committed yourself to a low rate of return. Of course, if the reverse happens and you lock in before rates plummet, you will congratulate yourself on doing the right thing. However, if the experts consistently make errors in their predictions of interest rate trends, the chances of you getting it right are slim.

Some form of inflation proofing is an essential element for most people in their income-generating portfolio of investments. The purchasing power of £100 will be worth just £64 after 15 years of inflation at 3 per cent and £48 if the inflation rate is 5 per cent.

The hidden cost of income guarantees is a reduction in the real purchasing power of your capital. As a rule, guaranteed income products limit, or exclude, any prospect of capital growth. With some products, part of your capital could be used to bolster income if returns are lower than expected. Exposure to this type of investment should be limited.

If investing for income *growth* is a better way of describing your requirements, you should include at least some equity investments within your portfolio. Clearly this introduces risk, but, provided you aim for diversity and avoid the exotic, your main concern will be fluctuations in income rather than the fear of losing everything.

Tax status

This is a crucial factor in your choice of savings products. For example, the income from National Savings Pensioners' Bonds is paid gross but the income from insurance company guaranteed bonds in effect is paid net of basic rate tax and you cannot reclaim this. In theory this should make the NS bonds a clear winner for non-taxpayers, but the slightly higher income available on the insurance bonds can offset this tax advantage. Depending on rates at the time, non-taxpayers should consider both products.

In the following pages we outline some of the most popular savings and investment options for income seekers – and one or two unusual opportunities you may come across in your research.

Income earners

National Savings

National Savings offers a wide range of accounts and bonds designed for every age and tax status. **Income bonds**, for example, have a three-month notice period for withdrawals and the bonds must be held for a minimum of one year. If you don't give the required notice you lose 90 days' interest.

NS Savings certificates can be either fixed rate or index linked and both run for five years. All returns are tax free, even with early repayment, although if you don't go the full five years the interest rate drops. NS **Pensioners' guaranteed income bonds** can be bought by anyone over 60 and offer a monthly tax-free income guaranteed for five years. NS also offers two accounts with a pass book – the investment account, which requires one month's notice, and the ordinary account, which offers instant access at post office counters.

One of the attractions of NS products is that you can buy them through the post office and there are no charges. Bear in mind though that NS changes its interest rates less frequently than building societies so you should always compare rates before committing yourself.

For details of the complete range of NS products, ask at your local post office or use the contact details provided at the end of this chapter. Remember, NS does not pay commission to advisers – which may explain why many commission-based advisers fail to recommend them.

Tax-exempt special savings accounts (Tessas)

Tessas were withdrawn for new investment after April 5, 1999, but if you have an existing account that is coming up to maturity you can reinvest the capital in a special Tessa-only Isa. The amount transferred does not count towards your annual Isa allowance.

Tessas were not specifically designed to generate income but it is possible to make partial withdrawals of the interest and retain the tax-exempt status. Most Tessas pay a variable interest rate, although a few providers offered a fixed rate for either one year at a time or for the full five years.

If your first account has matured, provided you act within six months of the maturity date you can transfer the capital (up to a maximum of £9,000) to the Tessa/Isa and enjoy a further five years' tax-free growth.

Cash individual savings accounts

Isas are discussed in more detail in Chapter 12. Part of your £7,000 annual subscription can be paid into a deposit account. This was £3,000 a year at the time of writing. You can hold this in a cash-only or mini-Isa, but if you take out one of these you can't invest the rest of your subscription in a separate equity Isa.

Despite the low maximum annual limit, the cash Isa is a tax-efficient way to boost your savings and for many investors the tax break on the mini Isa is more valuable than that associated with the equity maxi-Isa. This is because cash Isas give complete exemption from income tax on the interest, while investment Isas are still liable for some income tax on dividends, although they have a complete exemption from capital gains tax and no income tax is paid on bonds or bond funds.

Interest rates tend to be excellent on the top Isas (see *Moneyfacts* for the best rates), but keep an eye on providers that offer a special rate for just a few months in order to entice you in, then drop back to a much more mundane level of interest. If you are prepared to tie up your money, you can get an even better rate on notice accounts.

Watch out for inflexible clauses that penalize you if you want to transfer your fund elsewhere, for example. If you stick to CAT-marked Isas, the accounts must offer you instant access, among other features. CAT stands for charges, access and terms.

> **Watch out for inflexible clauses that penalize you if you want to transfer your fund elsewhere.**

Gilts and bonds

Gilt-edged stocks are bonds issued by the UK government via the UK Debt Management Office (DMO), an executive agency of the Treasury. If you buy gilts you are lending the government money in return for a tradable bond that promises to pay a fixed regular income for a specified period, at the end of which the government repays the original capital. Investors can buy and sell gilts throughout the lifetime of the issue.

Gilts play an important part in a defensive or income-producing portfolio, although investors might also look at corporate bonds to improve their yields.

The DMO website (see Further information below) is an excellent source of information for private investors and maintains an up-to-date list of all the gilts in issue. The most common category is the conventional gilt, which behaves like a conventional bond and pays interest twice a year. You can also buy index-linked gilts, which pay a dividend that rises each year in line with the retail price index. The third category listed – rump gilts – refers to issues where there are very few gilts in circulation (see Gilt jargon below).

Private investors can buy gilts in several ways. You can purchase through a bank or stockbroker that is a member of the Gilt Edged Market Makers Association (Gemma). If you buy and sell in this way the bank or stock-broker will charge a commission for the transaction. You can also buy through the Bank of England brokerage service direct (see Further information below) or via the post office.

Information on gilt prices and yields is published in the second section of the *Financial Times* on weekdays and in the first section on Saturdays.

Gilt jargon

Conversion: A conversion is where the Debt Management Office offers to exchange an existing gilt with a new issue. You don't have to accept the conversion but if you decide to hang on to your original issue it could end up as a rump and be hard to sell (see below). Don't confuse conversion with 'convertible'. There are no gilts with a convertible option in issue at present, but this refers to a type of gilt that allows you to exchange one issue for another at a predetermined date.

Floating rate: This type of gilt, which is not considered suitable for private investors, is designed to mirror eurobond floating rate notes and tracks the London Interbank Bid Rate (Libid).

Gilt strips: Here gilts are divided or stripped into their component parts – that is, the interest and redemption payments. The interest payments can be bought and sold separately and can be treated as a gilt in their own right. Gilt strips are regarded as a particularly sophisticated product and are more volatile than conventional gilts.

Rump gilts: This refers to issues where there are very few gilts in circulation, perhaps following a conversion (see above). The point to note about rump gilts is that liquidity can be a problem due to the small numbers.

Undated gilts: These gilts, also known as 'callable' gilts, have passed the redemption date set in the original prospectus. In most cases the DMO can give three months' notice to redeem undated gilts so in many ways they behave like a three-month bond.

How to assess bond income

To assess the income from gilts and bonds you need to look at three figures.

- The **nominal** value represents the original purchase price (which is not necessarily the price at which you buy). This is the amount you receive at redemption.
- The **coupon** tells you the interest rate that applies to the nominal value throughout the loan period.
- The **market price** is the present value if you buy or sell.

The coupon and nominal figures determine the level of interest, but the actual return or yield will depend on the buying price. If the buying or market price of a gilt or bond goes up, the yield goes down because you have paid more than the nominal value and therefore the interest rate will be smaller in comparison. So, if the nominal price is 200p and the interest rate is 10 per cent but you buy at 240p, the interest is still only 10 per cent of 200 – that is 20p, so the yield is 8.33 per cent (20p as a percentage of 240p).

If the situation is reversed, so the nominal is 240p, the interest rate 10 per cent and you buy at 200p, you will still get 10 per cent of 240p, which is 24p – a yield of 12 per cent.

Corporate bond funds and guaranteed income bonds

Historically, gilts have played an important part in the more defensive portfolio and particularly as a safe, interest-generating asset for the retired. However, given the low rates of interest currently on offer, many private investors are turning for a better return to corporate bonds (bonds issued by companies as opposed to the government).

There are risks, of course. Gilts are guaranteed by the government and are considered ultra secure. Corporate debt is guaranteed by companies. Some of it may be secured on assets but generally speaking the security is much lower than for government stock. This is reflected in the company's credit rating. To help investors assess the risk attached to a bond, leading credit rating companies such as Standard & Poor's and Moody's have established credit gradings. AAA is the highest grading and therefore bonds from these companies are considered the most secure. A very low credit stock – that is less than BBB – can have a very high yield. However, the potential for capital loss is equally high.

Two quite different ways to invest in corporate bonds are through collective funds, such as **corporate bond unit trusts** or insurance funds, and through **guaranteed income bonds** (GIBs). Corporate bond funds can be held in an Isa. Advisers do not recommend corporate bond funds for the short-term investor due to the buying and selling costs. They also suggest you should avoid bond funds that deduct the annual management charge from capital instead of income as this structure may be used to artificially inflate the potential yield. GIBs for the short term are very different animals. They are used as comparatively short-term investments, while corporate bond funds are medium to long-term investments. With a GIB your capital and income is guaranteed. Corporate bond funds offer potentially higher yields but neither the capital nor the income is guaranteed. Here it is vital to examine the underlying bonds held to achieve the yield and to check the charges.

A leading GIB provider such as AIG Life, for example, will invest in top-quality debt, including high quality corporate bonds, sterling eurobonds, sterling-denominated AAA government bonds, and World Bank AAA debt, among other instruments. Some of the bond funds that offer a higher yield achieve this by buying lower quality debt instruments which can expose the investor to greater risk.

Guaranteed income bonds offer a fixed rate of interest over a specific term. Most investors go for three years or less. You can invest anything from £5,000 and at maturity you get back your original capital plus interest, unless you elect to have interest paid out during the term of the bond.

In addition to the one to five-year bonds, AIG Life and GE Life offer 'odd-term' or made-to-measure GIBs for wealthy investors who need to fix for a specific period. AIG Life also offers variable rate accounts for those who need total flexibility of access, although obviously here the income is not guaranteed.

With such a variety of terms available, the made-to-measure bonds are considered ideal for two very different types of investor: risk-averse older people who need a regular income from savings, and wealthier individuals who want a first class cash-management system. The odd-term bonds are often used to hold cash set aside to pay large income and capital gains tax bills each year on January 31.

GIBs are a type of life assurance fund. The taxation of life assurance funds is complicated, but according to AIG Life, if you are a higher rate taxpayer, a deposit account rate of 5 per cent gross will actually yield £3 for every £100 invested, whereas the GIB will yield £3.28. Remember that GIB providers are forced to quote their rates net of basic rate tax whereas the banks and building societies quote gross rates. To compare like with like, a higher rate taxpayer will need to deduct 40 per cent from the building society rate and only 18 per cent from the GIB rate.

GIBs pay interest net of basic rate tax and if you are a non-taxpayer you cannot reclaim this. For this reason GIBs are generally considered unsuitable for non-taxpayers. However, since these bonds generally pay slightly higher rates of income than the tax-free NS products, it pays to consider both options.

A higher-rate taxpayer who owns a GIB can defer any additional liability until the end of the investment term. Furthermore, once a bond matures, if you want to reinvest your capital you can defer the tax liability if the insurance company issues a formal offer to you to reinvest the entire proceeds in a new bond.

Given the fluctuating yields on the underlying assets, GIB rates change frequently, so seek advice on the timing of your investment. Most GIB providers will only sell through independent financial advisers. The rates usually assume a commission payment, so where the adviser arranges for this to be reinvested, your income will be even higher.

Two other options that guarantee to return your original capital are **National Savings premium bonds** and **guaranteed equity bonds**. However, both are unsuitable for income seekers. In the case of premium bonds, no income is paid and you have to rely on the probabilities of winning to earn the equivalent of interest on your investment.

Guaranteed equity bonds use derivatives to guarantee a percentage of stock market growth or to guarantee the unit value of fully invested funds. A few of these funds offer to pay an income but only when the relevant index has achieved a specific return.

Halfway houses

Many investors, particularly pensioners, need to squeeze as much income as possible from their savings and are reluctant to take any risks with the capital. The trouble with this approach is that inflation eats into the real value of both capital and income. This is why most advisers recommend that income seekers should have at least a portion of equity-based invest-ments in their portfolios.

But if you genuinely believe you cannot afford the risk of ordinary shares it is worth considering a halfway house – that is, investments which offer some capital protection plus a rising income. This category of investments includes **index-linked gilts** and the **stepped preference shares of split capital investment trusts**.

Index-linked gilts

These bonds are issued by the government and guarantee to increase both the six-monthly interest payments and the 'nominal' or original capital investment which is returned to you on the redemption date. The capital increases in line with the retail prices index (RPI).

Since the starting RPI figure used is eight months before the date of issue, the final value of the investment can be calculated precisely seven months before redemption (RPI figures are published a month in arrears). But, as we discussed on page 63, guarantees offered by government or corporate bonds apply only if you hold the bonds to maturity. Like conven-tional gilts (see page 83), the index-linked variety are traded actively, so the price and real value can fluctuate significantly between the issue and redemption dates.

Investors seeking absolute guarantees from their income-yielding portfolios may be tempted to put all their money into gilts. In this case you might be better off with a balance between conventional gilts, which offer a comparatively high fixed income but no index-linking of the capital value, and index-linked gilts, which offer a low initial income but protect both the income and capital from rising inflation.

Stepped preference shares of split capital trusts

These are discussed on page 93, but briefly 'stepped prefs' offer an income which is guaranteed to rise each year at a fixed rate, and a fixed redemption price for the shares when the trust is wound up. Each trust offers a different yield and annual increase, depending on the nature of the underlying assets.

The factors to consider are the risk profile, the current dividend yield, and the gross redemption yield – that is, the total return expressed as an annual percentage, assuming the share is bought at the present price and held to maturity.

The best source of information on all types of investment trust is the Association of Investment Trusts (AITC), which publishes useful fact sheets and a Monthly Information Service, which provides a breakdown of all the member trusts and performance statistics. (For contact details, see page 237).

Purchased life annuities (PLAs)

Annuities, sold by insurance companies, guarantee to pay a regular income for life in return for your lump sum investment. The annuity 'rate' – or the level of regular income you secure in return for your lump sum – will depend on several important factors, including your life expectancy and interest rates. Women tend to live longer than men so usually receive a lower income in return for the same level of investment. If you are in ill health you may be able to get a better rate if the insurance company thinks your life expectancy is less than the average for your age. This is known as an ill health or impaired life annuity. The main point to remember with annuities is that unless you pay extra for a capital guarantee, once you hand over your money it is gone for good, even if you die the following day. Annuity rates are interest rate sensitive and fluctuate considerably, so seek expert advice over the timing of the purchase and the annuity company. For further details on PLAs, see page 207.

Summary

- Remember that many 'safe' investments do not protect your capital from inflation.
- Keep at least three times your monthly outgoings in an account which has one week's notice.

- Most income seekers are actually looking for income growth and therefore need an element of equity investment in their portfolio.
- Make sure the taxation of the product is suitable for your tax status.
- National Savings does not pay advisers sales commission.

Glossary of terms

Bonds and gilts are IOUs which offer a regular income and a return of your original capital at the maturity date. Gilts are issued by the government. A rising income is available through index-linked gilts. Guaranteed income bonds are sold by insurance companies.

Cash Isas have replaced Tessas. You can invest up to £3,000 of your £7,000 annual Isa allowance in a cash version.

National Savings certificates and bonds are backed by the government.

Purchased life annuities offer a guaranteed income for life in return for a lump sum investment.

Stepped preference shares of split capital investment trusts offer an income guaranteed to rise each year at a fixed rate.

Tax exempt special savings accounts (Tessas) are deposit accounts which offer tax-free returns if you hold the investment for five years. Tessas were withdrawn in 1999 but you can reinvest your capital in a special Isa.

Further information

Moneyfacts is available in larger libraries and by subscription. You can also buy a single copy by credit card – 01603 476476. Price at the time of writing was £5.95.

Visit the Debt Management Office website at **www.dmo.gov.uk**. The site includes an online version of the informative *Private Investors Guide*.

You can contact the Bank of England brokerage service on freephone 0800 818614 or go to the website at **www.bankofengland.co.uk**. A link appears on the DMO site.

For details of the complete range of National Savings products, ring 08459 645000 or visit the website at **www.nationalsavings.co.uk**.

Unit trusts, investment trusts, open-ended investment companies and insurance funds

This chapter describes the four most popular types of collective funds in the UK. Although these funds share many features in common and offer a similar broad investment scope, there are differences in structure and taxation. Your choice will depend on the finer details.

Unit trusts and open-ended investment companies

Although there are differences between the unit trust and open-ended investment companies (oeic) structure, as far as the private investor is concerned these two types of fund can be treated as identical. For the sake of simplicity, where we refer to a unit trust, this covers both products.

A unit trust is a collective fund with a specific investment aim. The trust can invest in a range of assets which are suitable for the relevant investment criteria, for example it can aim to produce an income through investing in higher yielding UK equities, or to generate capital growth through investing in new or expanding industries or, more riskily, in emerging markets.

> Unit trusts sold to the public are authorized by the chief financial services regulator, the Financial Services Authority (FSA).

Unit trusts sold to the public are authorized by the chief financial services regulator, the Financial Services Authority (FSA). (You may hear about another type – 'unauthorized' unit trusts are used as internal funds by financial institutions and are not marketed to the public.) Unit trusts are 'open ended', which means they may create or cancel units on a daily basis depending on demand.

Investors purchase units in the fund, the value of which fluctuates in line with the value of the underlying assets. In this respect a unit trust functions in a similar way to other collective funds (insurance funds for example), although the tax treatment for these two types of fund is quite different (see below).

Investment scope

Unit trusts can invest in 'transferable securities' (securities which can be bought and sold on the open market) listed on any market that meets the criteria set out in the European Union's Undertakings for Collective Investment in Transferable Securities (Ucits) directive. Basically, managers are free to decide which markets are suitable for their funds but they must ensure the markets operate regularly, are open to the public, and offer the appropriate levels of liquidity.

Most funds invest mainly or wholly in equities, although the number of corporate bond funds – which invest in corporate bonds, preference shares and convertibles, among other assets – is growing rapidly.

Some Isas (and previously, Peps) based on unit trusts offer capital guarantees or guarantee to provide part of the rise in a stock market index and protect you from the falls. The guarantee is 'insured' through the use of derivatives – financial instruments which are used to protect a fund's exposure to market fluctuations.

For the more cautious investor these 'protected' unit trusts, as they are called, when held within an Isa could represent a tax-efficient method of gaining a high exposure to equities without the usual risks. However, it is important to remember that protection carries a cost – in this case the price of the derivatives – which will be passed on to the investor through increased management charges. Some advisers argue that you might be better off gaining full exposure to an index through one of the low-cost index-tracking Isas and hedging your exposure to risk by investing part of your capital in gilts or National Savings, for example.

To date, the guaranteed fund market has been dominated by insurance companies with their popular guaranteed bonds. Insurance bonds are pooled funds similar in concept to unit trusts, but there are important differences that are discussed below.

Investment trusts

An investment trust is not a trust as such but is a British company, listed on the UK stock exchange, which invests in the shares of other quoted and unquoted companies in the UK and overseas. As public companies, investment trusts are subject to company law and Stock Exchange regulation. The prices of most investment trusts are published daily in the *Financial Times*.

Investment trusts are controlled by boards of directors who are appointed by and answerable to their shareholders. The board presents annual accounts to its shareholders.

Difference between investment and unit trusts

Investment trusts are different from unit trusts in several important ways and offer the active investor additional opportunities. However, these opportunities also make investment trusts potentially more volatile than unit trusts.

Investment trust companies have a fixed number of shares so, unlike unit trusts, 'units' cannot be created and cancelled to meet increased and reduced demand. As with any quoted company, the shares are available only when other investors are trying to sell.

This means there are two factors that affect investment trust share prices. The first is the performance of the underlying assets in which the company invests. This factor also affects the price of units in a unit trust.

However, where unit trust prices directly reflect the net asset value of the fund, investment trust share prices may not. This leads to the second factor, which is that the market forces (supply and demand) to which investment trust shares are subject may make the shares worth more or less than the underlying value of the company's assets. If the share price is lower than the value of the underlying assets, the difference is known as the discount. If it is higher, the difference is known as the premium.

Investment trusts can borrow money to invest, an activity known as gearing. This adds extra flexibility and if the shares purchased with the borrowed money do well, the company and its shareholders will benefit. A poor return on the shares will reduce the profitability of the company.

'Split capital' investment trusts can have two types of shares – one that has a right to all the income and one that has a right to the capital growth. There are several other types of share, each offering different features, for example stepped preference shares (see page 87) which offer dividends which rise at a predetermined rate and a fixed redemption value which is paid when the trust is wound up.

Taxation outside of an Isa or Pep

In terms of taxation, the unit and investment trust routes are very similar. Where these investments are held outside of an Isa (or a Pep), in both cases the capital gains tax liability falls on the investor who can offset any tax liability against the annual CGT exemption (£7,500).

There is no easy way to explain the taxation of dividends, so here's one we took from the *Financial Times*: dividends are taxed at 10 per cent up to the basic rate limit and 32.5 per cent thereafter. However, each dividend also comes with a tax credit (up to April 5, 2004) valued at 10 per cent of the grossed-up amount. This means that a basic rate taxpayer has no further tax to pay. Higher-rate taxpayers pay an additional 22.5 per cent. (See Chapter 12 for taxation within an Isa or Pep.)

Charges on investment trusts are generally lower than on unit trusts, with the exception of index tracker unit trust Isas/Peps. However, tracker funds available as Isas are confined to the UK stock market and therefore do not offer such broad diversification as the larger and older international investment trusts.

In conclusion, unit trusts, with the exception of the index trackers, are generally considered slightly more expensive than investment trusts but less sensitive to market movements.

Insurance funds

Like unit trusts, a lump sum premium in an insurance fund (also known as an insurance company bond) buys units, which directly reflect the net asset value of the fund's underlying investments. The charges for the two types of collective funds are broadly similar, although insurance company bonds may have slightly lower annual charges but tend to pay advisers higher rates of commission than unit trusts.

> There are circumstances in which the unique features of bonds can be attractive to higher rate taxpayers who may be able to defer or avoid a proportion of the tax generated by the fund.

However, the tax treatment is quite different. Insurance company bonds pay tax broadly equivalent to the basic rate on income and capital gains. The income tax cannot be reclaimed so, generally, these bonds are not considered suitable for non-taxpayers. Moreover, the capital gains tax paid by the fund cannot be offset against an individual's exemption. Experts tend to regard this feature as a serious drawback.

There are circumstances in which the unique features of bonds can be attractive to higher rate taxpayers who may be able to defer or avoid a proportion of the tax generated by the fund.

Despite the confusing array of investments offered by insurance companies to the public, most fall into one of three main categories:

■ **Maximum investment plans (MIPs)** are regular monthly or annual premium investments and usually run for ten years. Once this term is complete you can either take the proceeds or leave the fund to continue to benefit from investment growth. You can also make tax-efficient annual withdrawals.

■ **Insurance company investment bonds** are similar to MIPs but here you invest a single premium or lump sum.

■ **Endowments** combine investment with a substantial element of life assurance.

With maximum investment plans and insurance company investment bonds your premiums are invested in a choice of funds, most of which are unit linked, similar in concept to unit trusts in that your premiums buy units in a collective fund and the value of those units rises and falls in line with the value of the underlying assets.

Although sold by life assurance companies, most of these regular and single-premium plans offer minimal life cover as their main purpose is investment. If you die, the company might pay out 101% of your original investment or the value of the fund, whichever is greater.

The third category – the traditional endowment – is most commonly used as a repayment vehicle for a mortgage. (Endowment mortgages are discussed in more detail in Chapter 16.) As mentioned above, the distinguishing feature of an endowment is that it combines a significant element of life assurance with your savings plan so that if you die during the term of the policy the combination of the value of your fund plus the life assurance is sufficient to repay the debt.

In addition to the unit linked investment options you can also invest in with profits funds. With profits and 'unitized' with profits endowments invest in a mixture of equities, bonds and property and have a rather idiosyncratic method of distributing profits. The two types of with profits funds and the chief alternative – unit-linked funds – are discussed below.

Taxation of insurance funds

At the end of the investment period, the proceeds of an investment in an insurance fund (which is actually classed as a life assurance policy, will be treated as though the fund had already paid the equivalent of basic rate tax. For lower and basic rate payers that is the end of the story. But what happens next for higher rate payers depends on whether the policy is classed by the Inland Revenue as 'qualifying' or 'non-qualifying'.

With a qualifying policy there is no further tax liability for higher rate payers. However, to attract this special tax status the policy must abide by various conditions. First, it must be a regular premium plan where you pay a predetermined amount each month or each year. Second, it has to be a long-term plan – usually a minimum of 10 years. Third, it has to provide a substantial amount of life cover.

This means that single-premium investment policies are non-qualifying but the regular premium MIPs may be classed as qualifying depending on the term and level of life cover provided. Mortgage endowments, which tend to be long-term regular premium plans, usually qualify due to the substantial element of life cover.

The important point to note about life assurance policies is that the income tax cannot be reclaimed so, generally, these policies are not considered suitable for non-taxpayers. Moreover, the capital gains tax paid by the fund cannot be offset against an individual's exemption as is the case with unit and investment trusts. Financial advisers tend to regard this feature as a serious drawback.

Unique tax features of investment company bonds

There are some circumstances in which the unique features of investment bonds can be attractive to certain investors.

Annual withdrawals

With bonds there is no annual yield as such since income and growth are rolled up within the fund. But up to 5 per cent of the original capital can be withdrawn each year for up to 20 years. The Inland Revenue treats these withdrawals as a return of capital and therefore at the time of payment they are free of tax so the higher rate tax liability is deferred until you cash in your policy. (Withdrawals above 5 per cent are treated by the Inland Revenue as though they are net of basic rate tax, so the higher rate liability must be paid, not deferred.)

Higher rate taxpayers who have used their full CGT allowance may also find bonds and MIPs attractive because the 5 per cent withdrawals do not have to be declared for income tax purposes in the year of withdrawal.

Top slicing relief

Even if you invest in a non-qualifying life policy you may be able to reduce or avoid the deferred higher rate tax bill due to the effect of top slicing relief. Top slicing relief averages the profit over the number of years the bond has been held and adds this profit slice to an investor's income in the year the bond matures. If part or all of this falls into the higher rate bracket, it would be taxed. However, with careful tax planning, investors can avoid this liability by encashing the bond when they become basic rate taxpayers – in retirement, for example.

One advantage of bonds over most unit trusts is that insurance companies generally offer a low-cost switching facility between a large range of funds. Otherwise the charges for the two types of funds are broadly similar, although the tax status of life offices usually allows them to operate with slightly lower annual charges and this can have a significant effect on your fund's growth over the long term.

Investment choice

The investment choice under insurance funds (life assurance policies) is as follows.

'Unit linked' plans offer a very wide choice, ranging from UK and international equities to UK and international fixed-interest securities, index-linked gilts, property, and commodity and energy shares. Your money buys units in the fund's assets and the unit price rises and falls directly in line with the performance of these assets.

Clearly it is possible to select different types of fund depending on your preferred asset allocation, but for investors just starting out and for those with limited amounts to invest, a managed fund is ideal. Managed funds usually invest in a range of the company's core funds – for example a managed equity fund would invest in the company's main UK and international equity funds. Managed funds may also include different types of assets – for example equities and bonds – to provide a better balance of risk or to generate a higher income than could be achieved with a pure equity fund.

'With profits' funds are simply heavenly if you thrive on jargon and obscurity – which is a pity really because they can play an important role in a more cautious investor's portfolio. The with profits fund is the fund of the life office itself and invests mainly in a range of international and UK equities, bonds and property. The way the fund's profits are distributed resembles a cross between a building society deposit account and a unit-linked fund. Under the original structure for 'with profits – now known as 'conventional' with profits – you are guaranteed a 'basic sum assured' and each year an annual interest or 'bonus' is added to this sum (sometimes referred to as a 'reversionary' bonus). Once this has been added it cannot be taken away, although the rate for future years is not guaranteed. To avoid dramatic fluctuations, insurance companies 'smooth' their bonus rates, holding back some of their profits in the good years to maintain a reasonable return in the bad years.

In addition to the annual bonus you receive a final or 'terminal' bonus at the end of your investment period or when you die. The final bonus is discretionary (that is, voluntary on the part of the insurance company) and tends to reflect recent performance.

The more modern version – 'unitized' with profits funds – invest in the same assets but do not offer a basic sum assured. Also, unitized with profits funds have a feature which allows the insurance company to reduce the value of your units if there is a run on funds – after a market crash, for example. Most companies rarely use this 'market value adjuster' but its very existence means that your fund value is never totally guaranteed as Equitable Life policyholders have discovered.

However, in favour of unitized funds is the ease with which you can switch to and from unit-linked funds – an exercise that can be difficult with conventional with profits.

In recent years bonus rates have fallen, partly due to cuts in interest rates and partly to compensate for what many commentators regard as over-generous bonuses paid in the late 1980s. This does not mean that with profits policies represent poor value – some companies continue to achieve very good results over the medium to long term. However, it does mean that you cannot rely on bonus levels of the past to continue in future.

Distribution bonds, pioneered by Sun Life in 1979, are becoming an increasingly popular alternative to with profits due to their 'safety first' approach to investment. Unlike a typical managed unit-linked fund, which would be primarily invested in equities, distribution bonds tend to have a much higher proportion of bonds, gilts, deposits and property. In this way they cope well with most market conditions. They also tend to offer a higher yield than managed funds and so can be particularly attractive for investors seeking a regular income.

Friendly society policies

Friendly societies are often snubbed as the small fry of the investment industry. However, in contrast to life assurance funds, which have to pay both income and capital gains tax, friendly society funds are tax free.

> Friendly societies are often snubbed as the small fry of the investment industry.

Unfortunately, there are several drawbacks that detract from this attractive feature. First, the amount you can invest is small – £270 a year (£300 if you pay your premiums on a more regular basis than just once a year) and most plans run for ten years. There are societies that accept a lump sum investment to cover payments for the full ten years.

Second, the performance of some friendly society funds tends to be lacklustre but several offer good investment management and in some cases a link to one of the big institutional groups.

The third disadvantage is charges, which tend to be high in relation to the amount invested. However, again there are exceptions and several societies offer charges that compare well with individual savings accounts.

In conclusion, for small investments – perhaps for a child or grandchild – these plans can be worth considering. However, do look carefully at past performance and charges and compare these with what is on offer from Isa managers and unit and investment trusts which offer low-contribution regular savings plans.

Early surrenders and poor returns

Long-term life assurance investments tend to deduct the commission costs for the entire investment period during the first year or two. This is why so many people have got back so little from their policies if they have pulled out during this 'initial' period.

Your best bet is to avoid the commission structure altogether if you can by paying your adviser a fee and asking for the commission payments to be stripped out of the policy. Alternatively ask for a single-premium commission structure, where 4–5% is deducted from each premium throughout the entire term. This means that if you are forced to stop your policy during these early years, your fund should still have a reasonable value.

An endowment – or indeed any investment – is portable when it comes to mortgage repayment. If you buy another house and need a larger mortgage, keep the policy you have already and top up with a repayment or interest-only mortgage backed by the savings plan of your choice. You do not need to take out another endowment – an Isa may be a more tax efficient alternative if you are not already using up your annual allowance.

Beware of sales people who try to persuade you to surrender an existing investment in order to start a new policy for the whole of the mortgage. This almost certainly would lead to penalties and is bad advice.

Alternatives to surrendering a policy

If you simply cannot continue a policy for some reason, don't just stop payments without first considering the alternatives. You could, for example, make the policy 'paid up', which means you no longer pay premiums but you do not withdraw your fund until the maturity date. You should still benefit from investment growth, but check the ongoing charges and what penalties apply before taking this step.

If you need the capital, you might be able to take a loan from the insurance company, based on the surrender value of your policy. Alternatively, you might get up to 30 per cent more than the surrender value if you sell your policy on the second-hand endowments market. In this case an investor buys it from you and takes over the commitment to continue the premiums in the hope that the final payout will be well in excess of the purchase price plus the cost of the outstanding premiums.

The two main options are to auction the policy or to sell it to a market maker who, naturally, will charge a fee or take a percentage of the profit. (The profit is the difference between what you would have got as a surrender value from your insurance company and the actual price achieved.) See Further information below.

Alternative investments and hedge funds

Investments are described as 'alternative' where the risk and returns of the fund or asset do not correlate with (or behave in a similar way to) more traditional investments such as equities and bonds. Hence they are described as having a 'low correlation' with traditional equity and bond markets.

The most common example of an alternative investment is the hedge fund. Hedge funds aim to produce 'absolute' returns – that is, a positive return in all market conditions – and to eliminate market risk. The way they achieve this varies and the fund strategies are complicated.

The classic hedge fund picks undervalued stocks which the fund manager buys, and overvalued stocks, which the fund manager sells. The latter technique is known as 'short selling' and involves selling securities one doesn't own in order to buy them back at a lower price to return to the lender, while pocketing the profit. This basket of stocks that are sold short is the hedge or insurance against a fall in the markets. Not an easy concept.

While hedge funds may be an excellent idea in theory, in practice there are as many different styles as there are hedge fund managers. Some are indeed low risk but others are very risky, particularly where the fund borrows heavily, a process known as gearing. Advisers suggest that if you are interested in this type of investment approach you would be wise to start with a fund of hedge funds so that you spread risk across a range of managers. Several hedge funds can be held in an Isa.

Internet services

The Internet provides a huge source of information and it is also possible to buy funds and shares directly from a range of websites. We provide information on Internet services in Appendix 3.

Fund supermarkets are a big growth area. These sites allow you to mix and match different funds and fund managers within a single Isa. These sites are also provided in Appendix 3.

Offshore funds

In certain cases, for more wealthy, risk-tolerant investors it may be appropriate to consider offshore funds (but not before you have used up your annual Isa allowance). Whether an offshore fund would be suitable will depend on the tax jurisdiction of the fund, the way the fund itself is taxed and your own tax position as an investor. As a general rule for a UK investor investing in UK securities, once you have used up your Isa allowance, unit and investment trusts are likely to prove more cost effective and simpler than offshore funds.

Points to consider with offshore funds include the charges – which often can be very high compared with UK funds – and the regulation – for example, if it is outside the UK, what protection do you have if the company collapses or the fund manager runs off with your money?

There are two main types of offshore insurance bond – distribution bonds, which pay a regular 'income', and non-distribution bonds, which roll up gross.

Investors who may gain by going offshore include UK and foreign expatriates who are non-resident for UK tax purposes and who can benefit from gross roll-up non-distribution bonds if they do not pay tax in the country where they live. Higher rate taxpayers may also benefit from the gross roll up, but you have to pay tax when you bring the money back into the UK, although of course you may have switched to the lower tax bracket if you have retired by the time the non-distribution bond matures.

Summary

- The structure of investment trusts offers greater investment opportunities but at the same time greater potential risk than unit trusts.
- For most investors, particularly lower and basic rate taxpayers, unit and investment trusts are more tax efficient than insurance company funds. Some higher rate taxpayers can benefit from the insurance funds.
- The insurance companies offer a wider range of lower risk funds than unit trusts and allow for greater flexibility in switching.

- With profits funds are less risky than unit-linked funds but are also transparent.

- Unitized with profits funds offer a half-way house between the two products, but remember that there are fewer guarantees compared with the conventional with profits fund.

- Distribution bonds offer a careful mix of assets designed to help the fund withstand most market conditions and are therefore suitable for the more cautious investor, particularly income seekers.

- If you have an endowment and want to cancel, consider all your options – for example, you might do better if you sell it through the second-hand endowment market.

- Hedge funds aim to provide absolute returns – that is, a positive return throughout all market conditions – but they are very complicated and in many cases very risky.

- Unless there is a very good reason, don't go offshore.

Glossary of terms

Alternative investments do not follow the risk/return profile and pattern of traditional bond and equity markets.

Endowments combine investment with a substantial element of life assurance.

Hedge funds are a type of collective investment that aims to provide 'absolute' returns – that is, positive returns throughout all market conditions.

Insurance company bonds (or life assurance policies) are similar to unit trusts but the taxation is quite different.

Insurance company investment bonds are similar to MIPs but here you invest a single premium or lump sum.

Investment trusts are British companies that invest in shares of other companies in the UK and overseas. The share price does not necessarily reflect the value of the underlying assets.

Maximum investment plans (MIPs) are regular monthly or annual premium investments and usually run for ten years. Once this term is complete you can either take the proceeds or leave the fund to continue to benefit from investment growth. You can also make tax-efficient annual withdrawals.

Open-ended investment companies are similar to unit trusts but have a corporate structure.

Qualifying life assurance investment policies must follow certain rules but can pay the proceeds free of higher rate taxation.

Top slicing relief averages the profits of a policy over the term and adds the profit slice to your income in the year you take the proceeds. Investors who were higher rate taxpayers while saving but are basic rate taxpayers when they take the proceeds can avoid some or all of the higher rate liability.

Unit trusts are collective funds that can invest in a wide range of assets. The unit price reflects the underlying net asset value.

Further information

For further information on traded endowment policies (Teps), contact the Association of Policy Market Makers on 020 7739 3949, *www.money-world.co.uk/apmm*.

Individual savings accounts and personal equity plans

Personal equity plans

Over the 12 tax years – from January 1987 to April 1999 – that personal equity plans were available you could have invested a maximum of £85,000. After April 1999 you could no longer contribute to a Pep but any existing funds you had built up through your plan can remain in the tax-efficient wrapper and be managed as a separate portfolio.

Until April 5, 2001, there were two types of plan – general Peps and single-company Peps – and these two plans had to be kept separate. In the general Pep, after several changes to the rules, you could save up to £6,000 per annum and hold a range of collective funds. You could also use this annual allowance for a self-select Pep that allowed you to hold individual equities and bonds as well as collective funds. The single-company Pep, introduced in 1992, could be used to invest a further £3,000 per annum in the ordinary shares of a UK or EU listed company. Only one company's shares per annum were allowed.

This distinction has now been abolished so there is only one type of Pep and you are allowed to merge your investments. The government also lifted the geographical restrictions so that those who wish to do so can change their asset allocation to create a more international spread of investments.

In practice, many investors who took advantage of the Pep rules from the beginning are coming up to retirement and therefore may prefer to change the asset allocation to reflect an increased income requirement. Pep investors also have access to a wider range of corporate bonds and, for the first time, to gilts and other fixed-interest securities issued by European governments.

> In practice, many investors who took advantage of the Pep rules from the beginning are coming up to retirement and therefore may prefer to change the asset allocation to reflect an increased income requirement.

If you would like to make some changes to your Pep – including transfers to other managers – it is best to seek independent advice to make sure you fully understand the more flexible rules.

Individual savings accounts

Like Peps, Isas are not investments in themselves, but are simply Revenue-approved wrappers in which you can hold your investments. The range of investments is very flexible and includes a wide range of collective funds (see Chapter 11). You can also use a 'self-select' Isa to hold a portfolio of funds and individual shares and bonds. These are discussed below.

Clearly, if you have comparatively small amounts to invest it does not make sense to run your own portfolio because trading in small volumes is disproportionately expensive. For many investors, therefore, buying into collective funds through packaged Isas is cost effective.

Moreover, if you are happy to stick within a range of unit trusts and open-ended investment companies you can split your £7,000 allowance between several managers if you buy through a fund supermarket (see Appendix 3). This enables you to get round the one-Isa-per-year rule.

The Isa rules

Currently you can invest £7,000 a year in an Isa if you are 18 or over and a UK resident. There is no tax relief on the contribution but gains and income in the Isa fund build up free of tax. You do not pay tax on dividend income or interest. It is the fund manager's job to claim back the tax you are 'deemed' to have paid on all UK company dividends. Currently the credit is 10 per cent on share income, although this will be reduced to zero in 2004. You can get back 20 per cent on bond income. There is no capital gains tax liability for Isa investors (although this means you cannot offset a capital loss within an Isa against other gains).

There are two types of Isa plan, known as the mini and the maxi. You cannot take out both in the same tax year. You can invest in three separate mini Isas run by different managers. The limit is £3,000 in a cash mini Isa, £3,000 in shares and £1,000 in life assurance funds.

Alternatively you can take out a single maxi Isa with one manager and still invest in shares, cash and life funds but you can, if you wish, put the whole £7,000 into shares. Fund supermarkets allow you to invest across a range of managers within the single maxi plan.

CAT-marked Isas

As already mentioned, CAT stands for charges, access and terms. If you buy a CAT-marked product you are not guaranteed that it will be better than non-CAT-marked Isas but you can be sure the manager has agreed to certain conditions.

CAT-marked equity Isas
■ Annual management maximum charge of 1 per cent.
■ Minimum regular saving from £50 per month or a minimum lump sum of £500.

CAT-marked cash Isas
■ Must not have charges except for additional services, for example if you ask for an extra statement.
■ Must allow savers to pay in or withdraw as little as £10 on no more than seven days' notice.
■ Must not impose other conditions such as how frequently you can make withdrawals.
■ If interest rates go up, the Isa rate must follow within a month.

CAT-marked insurance funds
■ Maximum annual management charge of 3 per cent.
■ Minimum premiums from £25 per month or £250 per year.
■ Must not apply a penalty if you cash in your account.
■ When you surrender your account (cash it in) you must get back at least all the premiums you paid three years or more before the date when you cash in.

Self-select Isas

However, if you want maximum flexibility, the facility to invest directly in equities and bonds, and access to the full range of unit trusts, oeics and investment trusts in your collective Isa funds, you need a self-select plan. Self-select Isas are offered by many firms of stockbrokers (the Association of Private Client Investment Managers' website is at *www.apcims.co.uk*) and a few independent financial advisers, for example certain members of the Association of Solicitor Investment Managers (*www.asim.org.uk*).

Apart from the wider investment choice, one of the immediate benefits of the self-select structure is that it enables you to make changes to your portfolio on the same day. With packaged Isas it can take weeks and sometimes even months to switch between managers. This can be frustrating and costly in a rising market. You can also hold cash within the self-select plan and earn interest on this while you are waiting to reinvest the money.

This cash facility is particularly attractive if you want to make use of your Isa allowance but are concerned about the jittery markets and would rather wait a few months before making your investment decision. Also, dividends can be reinvested in the investment of your choice within the Isa, whereas if you invest with just one unit or investment trust manager, for example, any dividends earned must be reinvested with that manager or taken as tax-free income.

The main perceived disadvantage of the self-select route is the cost. If you buy a single packaged Isa, the plan costs are included in the standard charge. The cost of the Isa wrapper for unit trusts and oeics purchased through a fund supermarket is paid for by the fund managers out of their annual management charge. With the self-select plan the charge is in addition to your investment costs.

However, charges on packaged Isas are not necessarily as low as they seem. Even where the initial charge is discounted you are likely to find that your adviser receives 'trailer' commission. This is an annual charge, typically 0.5 per cent, which is deducted from your fund from year two onwards.

The cost of your self-select plan will depend on the stockbroker or adviser's charges. This might be a flat annual administration charge, which could suit the larger portfolios, or the fee might be linked to the value of the fund (for example 0.5 per cent per annum plus vat). Some will have no annual fees but will charge for dividend collection, which, on a large portfolio, could add up quickly. One thing to look out for is high dealing charges, especially on shares. What can appear cheap because of a low or zero annual management charge can prove costly if there is little or no discount on unit trust purchases and if sharedealing charges for buying and selling are in excess of 1 per cent.

Finally, don't forget that the self-select route can provide you with as much or as little advice as you want depending on whether you opt for a discretionary service, where your stockbroker makes all the investment decisions for you, an advisory service, where you and your stockbroker discuss your options before you make a decision, or execution only, where you make all the decisions yourself and your stockbroker simply carries out your instructions.

How to choose a self-select

It is important to shop around for your self-select plan to ensure you get the right type of service for your needs. For example, if you want to run your own portfolio and are happy to buy and sell on an execution-only basis, you might consider a plan offered by an Internet broker. However, if you want a discretionary or advisory stockbroker you need a firm with a full range of services.

Most stockbrokers offer a self-select Isa to existing clients as part of their overall portfolio management service but very few are available on a standalone basis, so your choice of plan may be dictated by your choice of stockbroker.

An alternative to the stockbroker route is to invest a nominal sum in an investment trust that also offers a self-select plan. The best example of this arrangement is the Alliance Trust, which provides a free administration service through its subsidiary Alliance Trust Savings, and access to a wide range of equities, investment trusts, corporate bonds, gilts and other collective funds. The only requirement is to invest £50 with either Alliance Trust or the 2nd Alliance Trust. Dealing charges for the two trusts are just £1 plus stamp duty. Charges for other transactions vary and are not as swift as an execution-only service.

> It is important to shop around for your self-select plan to ensure you get the right type of service for your needs.

Summary

- UK residents aged 18 and over can invest £7,000 in an Isa.

- Any investments held in a personal equity plan will retain their tax-exempt status. There is no capital gains tax on investments held within an Isa or a Pep. There is a limited amount of tax relief on dividends.

- The Isa allowance cannot be carried over to the following tax year.

- There are two types of Isa plan, known as the mini and the maxi. You cannot take out both in the same tax year. You can invest in three separate mini Isas run by different managers. The limit is £3,000 in a cash mini Isa, £3,000 in shares and £1,000 in life assurance funds.

- Alternatively you can take out a single maxi Isa with one manager and still invest in shares, cash and life funds but you can, if you wish, put the whole £7,000 into shares.

- CAT-marked Isas must offer low charges, easy access and fair terms.

- Fund supermarkets allow you to invest across a range of managers within the single maxi plan.
- Self-select plans allow you to hold any combination of funds and individual bonds and equities.

Glossary of terms

Advisory management is where you and your manager discuss investment decisions and the manager cannot act without your approval.

Corporate bonds are issued by companies that want to borrow money. The companies pay a fixed rate of interest and repay the capital on a specified date.

Dividends are part of the company's profits which are distributed every 6 or 12 months to shareholders.

Discretionary management is where your plan manager makes all the investment decisions for you.

Equities represent an investor's 'share' in the company's ownership – including its profits. To issue shares a company 'goes public' and is quoted on the Stock Exchange (the main exchange for UK companies) or the Alternative Investment Market (an exchange for smaller companies).

Execution only is where you make all the investment decisions and your stockbroker simply buys and sells on your instructions. No advice is provided.

chapter thirteen

Employee share ownership

Employee share ownership can bring excellent rewards and, with the general schemes, at little or no risk until you decide whether to buy. Buying shares through a company scheme is also tax efficient if you make a capital gain above the annual exemption as these shares are classed as business assets and the rate of CGT can be as low as 10 per cent (see page 47).

The best source of information on the range of company share schemes is ProShare. Contact details are provided at the end of this chapter and most of the material that follows was drawn from its publications.

There are more than 5,000 companies in the UK with approved employee share schemes, with about 3.5 million participating employees enjoying the tax benefits.

Currently, there are three Inland Revenue approved share schemes.

- ShareSave is the most popular, with over 1.75 million participants and more than 1,200 schemes in place.
- Profit-sharing schemes have around 1.25 million participants and 900 schemes in place.

Both of these schemes are all-employee share schemes, which means that all employees must be offered the opportunity to participate.

- Company Share Option Plans, or CSOPs, have 450,000 participants in over 3,750 schemes. This scheme has discretionary eligibility, which means that companies may choose which employees they would like to participate.

The government has introduced two additional share schemes:

- The New All-Employee Share Plan (AESOP)
- The Enterprise Management Incentives Plan (EMI).

In addition to the approved schemes above, companies may offer 'unapproved' share schemes. Although these do not offer the tax relief available under the approved schemes, they do offer more flexibility in design, which means that companies can create a bespoke scheme to meet their needs.

In this chapter we focus on the most popular arrangement, the ShareSave.

ShareSave (save as you earn)

The ShareSave scheme is also known as the Save As You Earn (SAYE) or Savings-Related Share Option Scheme, and was introduced under the 1980 Finance Act. There are currently over 1,200 approved ShareSave schemes in operation according to the Inland Revenue, with 1.75 million participants.

General features

> While you are saving you are in a 'no lose' situation. If the share price falls to below the option price, there is no requirement to exercise the options.

Under a ShareSave scheme employees have the right (known as an 'option') to buy shares at a future date at a price fixed shortly before the options are granted. The company can discount the price of the shares by up to 20% off the market value.

Shares can only be purchased with the proceeds of savings made under a special SAYE savings contract, set up with a bank or building society for a period of three or five years. The length of the option can be three, five or seven years. For the seven-year option, savings are made for five years only, but the money remains in the account for a further two years. Savings are made by payroll deduction from employees' net salary.

The benefits

While you are saving you are in a 'no lose' situation. If the share price falls to below the option price, there is no requirement to exercise the options. Instead you can simply take the proceeds of your savings contract plus the tax-free bonus at maturity (see below).

Who is eligible?

The scheme has to be open to all eligible employees of the company. A qualifying period of employment can be set but this must be no greater than five years. The majority of companies operating a ShareSave scheme have a much shorter eligibility period.

You can save between £5 and £250 per month. At maturity (the three, five or seven year anniversary from the contract start date if no payments have been missed), a tax-free bonus is paid. However, you lose the option to purchase shares if you close the savings account and withdraw your money before the end of the period of the contract. In this case the payments would attract interest at a rate of 3 per cent as long as the account was open for more than one year.

Also, if you miss more than six of the monthly contributions, the savings contract is effectively closed and the money returned to you. In this case the option to purchase shares would also lapse.

Buying the shares

At the maturity of the option, you have six months in which to exercise your right to buy. However, there is no obligation to purchase the shares. Your choices are as follows:

■ close the account and take the savings plus the tax-free bonus; or

■ close the account and use all of the proceeds to take up the option to purchase shares; or

■ close the account and take up the option in part (funds not used for the purchase of shares would be returned to the employee).

If you have missed any monthly payments (up to a maximum of six), the maturity date will be extended by the corresponding number of missed payments.

Income tax

There is normally no tax liability when you buy the shares. However, in the event of an early exercise of options (for example if the company you work for is taken over or sold) within three years from the date of granting the option, you may have to pay income tax on any gain.

Capital gains tax

If you sell the shares, there may be a liability to CGT on the gain between the sale price and the exercise price. (See page 47 for more details about CGT.) If you have been unlucky enough to make a loss on the shares, you can also offset this loss against any other gains you have made in that tax year.

Transfers to individual savings accounts

From April 6, 1999, shares released from the scheme can be transferred into an Isa. The value of the shares transferred will depend upon the year you want to make the transfer and the type of provider. For example, you could go to one Isa provider for the whole plan (a maxi Isa) or to separate providers for each component (a mini Isa). For more details about Isas see Chapter 12.

What happens if you leave the company?

If you change jobs and leave your current employer, you can no longer exercise the options. You can either carry on saving and take the cash and bonus at the end of the savings period, or close the account and take the payments made together with any interest, which is paid at 3 per cent per annum. However, employers have considerable discretion with these arrangements, so check the rules for your particular scheme.

If you leave due to special circumstances – for example redundancy, injury or disability – you have six months in which to exercise the option to buy from the date of leaving, using the amount saved plus any interest. If an employee dies, the option may be exercised by the personal representatives. In these circumstances, the option must be exercised in the 12 months following the death of the employee, or the maturity date, whichever is earlier. If the personal representatives do not exercise the option, the employee's savings, plus any bonus or interest due, will be paid to the estate.

Company share option plans (executive plans)

The main alternative to SAYE is a company share option plan, which in 1995 replaced the discretionary share option scheme. These were, and still are, commonly referred to as executive share option schemes because they are often open only to executives and directors. The plans are not linked to a savings contract, so you have to use spare capital to purchase.

Under the plan you do not pay income tax on the grant of an option or on any increase in market value of the shares in the period before you exercise the option. You can purchase the shares between three and ten years after the option was granted. Once you have made a purchase you have to wait another three years before you can exercise a further option to buy. Given the long period in which you have to choose, you might wish to take advice on when the experts consider the price is right.

The new schemes are not as attractive as the old executive schemes where the shares could be offered at a discount of up to 15 per cent and the maximum value of options per employee was the greater of £100,000 or four times salary. With the new plan the shares cannot be offered at a discount and there is a limit of £30,000 on the value of all the shares on option held by an employee.

Unapproved schemes

Some companies run 'unapproved' executive share option schemes. These do not offer the tax advantages of company share option plans but in theory there is no limit to the size of the option. However, options granted from November 27, 1996 will, on exercise, be subject to income tax under the Pay As You Earn (PAYE) system. This leads to difficulties if the employee's income tax charge is so large that it exceeds his salary and the company is unable to deduct it from monthly pay.

Profit-sharing schemes

You might also come across a profit-sharing scheme. Until April 2001 employers could set up a trust to give you an immediate gift of tax-free shares equivalent to a proportion of profit. The shares remain in the name of the trustees.

The maximum limit in value per employee is the greater of £3,000 a year or 10 per cent of annual salary, subject to a ceiling of £8,000. Provided you do not sell the shares before the end of the third year after allocation, there is no income tax to pay, although there may be a capital gains tax liability.

Summary

- Company share schemes offer you the opportunity to buy shares in your employer at a discount and in a tax-efficient manner.

- There are over 1,200 ShareSave schemes in operation. This is the most popular and common scheme.

- Shares usually are purchased with the proceeds of a regular savings scheme that runs for three, five or seven years.

- If the share price falls below the option price you can take the proceeds of your saving scheme and, if you complete the full term, a bonus is paid at maturity.

- Senior employees may be offered a different type of scheme that requires you to buy shares out of capital.

- Some executives are offered shares as a long-term incentive. This type of scheme may link the option to the company's perrformance.

Further information

Your employer should provide clear details of the various ways you can buy shares in the company. You can also contact your local Inland Revenue office for leaflets on the subject. These may be available in bank and building society branches.

A useful guide to employee share ownership is published by ProShare. Contact ProShare, Library Chambers, 13–14 Basinghall Street, London EC2V 5BQ. The website, at *www.proshare.org*, covers all the main arrangements.

Glossary of terms

Company share option plan (executive plan) is not linked to a savings contract – so you have to use spare capital to purchase. Under the plan you do not pay income tax on the grant of an option or on any increase in market value of the shares in the period before you exercise the option.

Profit-sharing scheme: Until April 2001 employers could set up a trust to give you an immediate gift of tax-free shares equivalent to a proportion of profit.

ShareSave (save as you earn) offers you the right to buy shares at a future date at a price fixed shortly before the options are granted.

Unapproved executive share option schemes do not offer the tax advantages of company share option plans but in theory there is no limit to the size of the option.

Saving for long-term projects: education fees and mortgage repayments

chapter fourteen

Saving for school and college fees

An increasing number of parents send their children to fee-charging independent schools. The reasons for so doing vary. In many cases, the parents are seeking academic excellence and the greater attention given to children through the benefit of smaller classes. Parents may have views on the 'traditional values' upheld by certain schools, or a child may have special needs or a particular talent which would flourish with the right type of guidance.

Whatever your reasons, sending your children to public school is a major financial commitment and should not be undertaken lightly. If you cannot afford to pay for private schooling out of your income and/or capital, and yet you are concerned about the standard of local state schools, one option is to move to an area with a better reputation. However, if you decide to move to a place with better state schools, first check the schools' admissions policy. By law you have the right to apply to any school, although there is no guarantee you will get a place. If a school is very popular and its priority for admissions is brothers and sisters of existing pupils, rather than local catchment area, you still might not qualify automatically for a place. The admission rules are explained in a prospectus which each school must provide free on request.

> Whatever your reasons, sending your children to public school is a major financial commitment and should not be undertaken lightly.

Even if you are happy with the local state junior and secondary schools, don't forget further education and university costs. Student grants have

FINANCIAL SNAPSHOT

There are almost 2,500 schools in Britain which are independent of local and central government control.

been abolished and if you want to put your children through university without landing them in debt, this is likely to cost about £7,000 a year – more if you live in London.

School fees

What does it cost?

For those who want private schooling for their children, planning ahead for school fees is essential, and that means starting when the children are toddlers, preferably babies. School fees vary considerably, but the following figures, provided by the Independent Schools Information Service (Isis), will give you a rough idea of the costs *per term*:

- Junior/preparatory (age 7 to 13): Day £1,200 to £2,500; Boarding £2,500 to £4,000

- Senior girls (age 11 to 18): Day £1,600 to £2,900; Boarding £2,900 to £5,000

- Senior boys (age 11 to 18): Day £1,600 to £3,500; Boarding £3,100 to £5,000

These figures are based on the 1999–2000 school year. In addition, you should find out about the cost of the uniform (this can be substantial), extra-curricular activities, and any other payments – for example, for examinations, lunches, school trips and so on. Isis reckons all of this could add up to 10 per cent to your bill.

> Senior boys' boarding schools can cost anything between £3,100 and £5,000 per term.

In practice, few parents aim to pay the total cost from savings. Grandparents often contribute to their grandchildren's education, and an injection of capital in the early years could make viable what initially appears to be an unrealistic savings plan. Many senior schools, and a few junior schools, offer scholarships to particularly bright children, although these rarely cover the full costs. Further financial help may be offered through a bursary, which is a grant from the school to help with the fees. These details are provided in the Isis directory.

What is a school fees plan?

Despite the dedicated packages put together by financial institutions and firms of advisers, all that a successful school fees plan does is provide good cashflow management backed by a range of suitable investments. To construct the right portfolio of investments for your circumstances, you need to know what the fees will be and the initial investment period before payments start.

You also need to factor in school fees inflation, salary inflation (if you intend to fund partly from income), and a sensible annual investment return. If you have some capital to invest at the outset and/or are prepared to pay part of the fees from income, clearly this will reduce the level of your regular savings.

If you want help with this exercise, seek genuinely independent advice. If you go to just one insurance company, with the aid of fancy software, you will be shown how you can achieve your goal if you invest mainly or wholly in insurance company products. You should also be cautious about plans and trusts that are linked to particular schools, as these may prove inflexible if you change your mind about the school. As a last resort, you could even tap in to the equity in your house or arrange an unsecured loan, but experts warn parents to think very carefully before taking this drastic step.

Which investments?

As the previous chapters have explained, the first and most important consideration is your attitude to risk, since this will define the type of portfolio and which funds you select. The tax status of both parents must also be taken into consideration, as must the time frame.

The last point is important because whichever investments you choose, your plan must cater for phased disinvestment to provide the regular drawdown for fees. You should also take out insurance to cover a regular savings plan, so it can continue if you die or become disabled and can no longer save. A combination of life assurance and critical illness insurance, which pays a lump sum on diagnosis of a major illness, might be suitable (see Chapters 2 and 3).

For the medium to long term, most advisers recommend parents use their annual Isa allowance (£7,000 each). Once you have used up your Isa allowance, then a combination of unit trusts, investment trusts and, possibly, insurance company bonds would provide a good exposure to equities, gilts and bonds through collective funds. If you have a capital lump sum to invest, and just a few years before you need to pay fees, a risk-averse investor might consider deposits in zero-coupon preference shares or gilts. Cash Isas and National Savings are also suitable where there are only a few years in which to save.

Finally, do make full use of your annual allowances and exemptions (see Section 3). For example, where one of the partners does not work, investors might consider transferring sufficient low-risk savings to the non-working spouse in order to make use of the annual personal allowance for income tax.

What next?

Many independent schools require prospective pupils to pass the Common Entrance Examination which is usually taken at age 11, 12 or 13. You can find out more details about the exam from the Independent Schools Examination Board. Although the exam is set centrally, the papers are marked by the school to which you have applied and each school has its own pass mark to ensure your child will be able to cope with its specific academic standard.

The Common Entrance Exam is broadly in line with the National Curriculum. However, Isis points out that independent preparatory schools spend the last two years preparing pupils for the exam, so clearly this gives children from independent schools a head start. If your child attends a state junior school, you should find out if there are specific subjects covered where private coaching would help your child to pass.

Isis publishes an annual directory of about 1,300 independent schools throughout the UK and Eire. Before you start to look around, the organization suggests you consider the following points to narrow down the choice:

- Day or boarding?
- Senior, junior or both?
- Single sex or co-educational?
- Academic or special requirements?
- Religious requirements?

All schools publish a prospectus, and some even produce a video to give you a more detailed impression of the school. Nothing serves so well as a visit, though, when you can make up your own mind about the head, the staff, the facilities and the pupils. The Isis directory provides a useful checklist of questions you might ask. One particularly good suggestion is to try to speak to the parents of existing pupils – probably the best reference you can get.

Further education costs

The government pays about three-quarters of the fees for university education. Typically, a full-time course would cost about £4,000 a year and the government puts around £3,000 towards it. This means you or your children have to cover the remaining contribution to tuition fees (unless you are a low earner) and living costs.

As a result, if you want your children to go to university or college, it is likely to cost about £7,000 a year – more if the university is in London. Students can borrow most of this through the Student Loans Company at preferential interest rates. If your children take out a loan, they have to start repayments in the April after they have finished college (earlier if they drop out). This is provided they earn more than around £10,000 a year (until then they don't have to make repayments).

The local education authority (LEA) handles the applications for tuition fee support, student loans and supplementary grants. You can find the number in the phone book under your local council.

Summary

- If you cannot afford to pay for private education, one option is to move to an area with a better reputation for state schools.
- Even if you are happy with the local state junior and secondary schools, don't forget further education and university costs.
- Find out about all the extras – the cost of the uniform, lunches, school trips, etc. could add an extra 10 per cent to your bill.
- Some schools offer scholarships, although they rarely cover the full cost.
- A school fees plan is simply a cash management exercise backed by suitable savings and investments.
- Make sure your plan is flexible.

Further information

Isis (Independent Schools Information Service), tel 020 7630 8793. For the website go to **www.isis.org.uk**.

Department for Education and Employment, Mowden Hall, Staindrop Road, Darlington, Co. Durham DL3 9BG. For *Financial Support for Students*, call freephone 0800 210 280 or visit website **www.dfee.gov.uk**.

For the free booklet on career development loans phone 0800 585 505 between 9am and 9pm Monday to Friday. Alternatively you may need to call the Student Awards Agency for Scotland on 0131 476 8212; the Department of Education for Northern Ireland on 01247 279279; or the Welsh Office Education Department on 01222 825831.

NHS bursaries: Contact your college or one of the following, depending on where you are studying: England – the NHS Student Grants Unit, tel 01253 856123; Wales – the Welsh Health Common Services Agency, tel 01222 825111; Scotland – the Student Awards Agency for Scotland, tel 0131 476 8212; Northern Ireland – Department of Education for Northern Ireland, tel 01247 279279.

National Union of Students, 461 Holloway Road, London N7 6LJ, tel 0207 272 8900, website ***www.nus.org.uk***.

Scottish Office Education Department: Phone for copies of *Investing in the future: Supporting students in Higher Education*, 0131 556 8400.

Social security: Ask your Department of Social Security for leaflet FB 23 *Young people's guide to social security*.

Student Loans Company Ltd: if you need to check the progress of your loan application, contact the Student Loans Company at 100 Bothwell Street, Glasgow G2 7JD or telephone freephone 0800 405 010.

Student information: Try ***www.studentpages.com*** for details of entertainment, shopping and money-saving facilities around UK universities. Plus how to join a freshers' service that offers free advice.

Tunbridge Wells Equitable is a friendly society that provides savings schemes for university fees. It offers some good generic advice and a ready-reckoner to calculate the monthly savings you need to make depending on your children's ages and your anticipated return. Go to ***www.twefs.co.uk***.

Introduction to mortgage planning

Most people would like to own their homes but finding the best way to achieve this can be daunting, not just for the first-time buyer but also for those who have taken a wrong turning and ended up in the negative equity trap, or with a completely inappropriate mortgage package. Untangling these complex problems can be an expensive and painful process, so it is worth spending time at the outset to get it right first time around.

There are plenty of sources of advice on mortgages and home ownership but probably the best guide to the basics is published by the Council of Mortgage Lenders (CML). *How to Buy a Home* is free and was the main source of information for this chapter (see Further information at the end of this chapter). The CML is a central body for the various types of mortgage lender – the banks, building societies, finance houses, insurance companies and specialist mortgage companies. For information on mortgage protection insurance, see Chapter 3, page 29. The Association of British Insurers (ABI) also publishes free fact sheets on mortgage protection and building and contents insurance.

Who can help?

When you decide you want to buy, your first step is to find out what you can afford, through a combination of any savings you already hold and by taking out a loan – a mortgage. How to find the right type of mortgage is the chief subject for this and the following chapter, but it may help to recap briefly on the various stages in the process of home purchase. This process in Scotland is different in some important respects, so if you are buying or selling north of the border, ask the CML for its guide *How to Buy a Home in Scotland*.

> When you decide you want to buy, your first step is to find out what you can afford, through a combination of any savings you already hold and by taking out a loan – a mortgage.

But first, a word on independent financial advice. Most people can see the sense in approaching an independent financial adviser for a personal pension or any other long-term investment, yet when it comes to the mortgage, the inclination is to think in terms of the lender first. In fact, the days when you had to have a building society deposit account for several years and prove your worth as a saver before being granted the privilege of a mortgage are long gone.

These days, provided you have a stable income, there is a huge range of mortgage facilities available and an independent adviser will have access to all the latest offers. He will also be able to warn you about the drawbacks of some of the special deals – for example, early repayment penalties or lack of flexibility if you want to top up the mortgage at a later date when you move to a larger house. Given the ease with which advisers can identify the best mortgages, your time will be better spent considering how you intend to repay the loan.

As with the mortgage itself, the range of repayment options has developed considerably in recent years, and some lenders require little more than a verbal assurance that you *will* save one way or another in order to repay the debt. If you opt for an interest-only mortgage backed by an investment plan – most commonly an individual savings account or possibly an endowment (but see page 138) – you are on pure investment ground and certainly need independent advice. Most building societies and banks offer a very limited range of options because they are 'tied' to one life office – increasingly their own. For a discussion on the merits of independent advice, read Chapter 1. For an examination of the main investment links, read Chapter 11.

Once you have established the amount and have found a house you can afford, you will make a formal offer and apply for the loan. The lender will insist on a valuation to check that the house is priced correctly. This is not the same as a structural survey, which is strongly recommended. It is far better to know where the woodworm and dry rot are before you hand over your money.

You may also be asked to provide evidence of your ability to keep up any previous mortgage payments, or evidence of regular rent payments.

FINANCIAL SNAPSHOT

A new code of practice for mortgage lending, introduced in 1997, should help ensure you get the best deal – but you cannot rely on it.

The mortgage lender will offer you an advance and if the conveyancer, who looks after the legal side of the process, is satisfied that all is in order, you will proceed to exchange of contract. This is when you make a formal commitment to buy, and the owner of the house makes a formal commitment to sell. At this stage, usually you are asked to pay a deposit of up to 10 per cent of the selling price to the conveyancer. A few weeks later on completion, when you take ownership of the house, you must pay the balance.

If you sell your main home, the proceeds are free of capital gains tax.

How much can you borrow?

Lenders differ in the amount they will offer, but broadly this will be up to three times your annual earnings, less any existing commitments such as hire purchase agreements and other outstanding liabilities. If you want a joint mortgage, the multiple is likely to be three times the higher income plus once the other income or up to two and a half times the joint income. The lender will want to see confirmation of your income – either a letter from your employer or, if you are self-employed, audited accounts for several previous years.

Clearly the amount of debt you can comfortably manage will depend on your circumstances. For example, even if you have two decent incomes now, it would make sense not to over-commit yourself if you plan to start a family in the near future and expect one of your incomes to substantially reduce or disappear for a few years.

Your mortgage and any capital you set aside from savings towards the house purchase need to cover several items other than the price of the house itself such as surveys, conveyancing fees, stamp duty, land registry fees and the removal costs.

Stamp duty is a government tax on the purchase of properties and must be paid where the purchase price exceeds £60,000. The current rate is 1 per cent on the full price, where this exceeds £60,000, 3 per cent for purchases between £250,000 and £500,000, and 4 per cent for purchases above this level. Land registry fees must also be paid for either registering the title to the property or the transfer where the title has already been registered. The fee for a £100,000 – £200,000 house was £200 at the time of writing.

You will also need to consider buildings and contents insurance, life assurance and, depending on existing cover, a payment protection policy.

What is a mortgage?

A mortgage is the legal charge on your property which you give to the lender in return for the loan – a sort of IOU if you like. Together with any special terms and conditions, the mortgage 'deed' is the legal contract between you and the lender. The CML guide explains that the most important features are:

■ the names of the parties to the contract, that is the borrower and the mortgage lender

■ the amount of the loan and your acknowledgement of receipt of the loan

■ a promise by you to repay the loan, with interest, on the stipulated terms. These include the amount of the initial repayments and any special terms, for example a fixed rate or a discount off the lender's variable rate for the first two years

■ the granting of the legal charge of the property to the mortgage lender until the loan is repaid

■ your commitment, if applicable, to any insurance policies and to carry out any repairs and alterations. For example, the lender may insist the house is re-roofed within the first three months of ownership to maintain the property's value.

> If you breach the terms of your mortgage contract – for example by failing to keep up the monthly payments – the lender has the power to take possession of the property and to sell it in order to recoup the loss.

If you breach the terms of your mortgage contract by failing to keep up the monthly payments, the lender has the power to take possession of the property and to sell it in order to recoup the loss. Repossessions are a last resort, but unfortunately they were an all too familiar feature of the late 1980s and early 1990s when many borrowers had over-stretched themselves and could not keep pace with rising interest rates.

The mortgage code

When you seek advice about your mortgage options make sure you use companies that follow the CML Mortgage Code. This is a voluntary code of practice but any reputable organization should adhere to it. The code protects you against poor practice. Lenders and brokers who follow the code must belong to an independent complaints scheme that can put things right if you have a valid complaint.

The government is considering regulating the information you must receive when you take out a mortgage in the future, but in the meantime you only have the protection of this code if you use a lender or broker who follows it, so do check.

Under the code your adviser or lender should give you a copy of the leaflet *You and your mortgage*, either at your first interview or as part of an information pack.

Lenders and advisers should tell you what they can offer you, including:

■ advice and a recommendation on which mortgage to choose

■ information on a range of deals to help you make up your mind; or

■ information only on a single deal if they offer only one type of mortgage or if you have already made up your mind.

If you go direct to a lender, obviously you will be offered only that company's mortgages. An independent adviser or mortgage broker, however, should be able to offer you a wide choice, although some will have links with specific companies and this may severely restrict your options. Under the code they should tell you:

■ whether they are acting independently for you or on the lender's behalf

■ which lenders they normally use

■ how much the lender will pay the broker for arranging the mortgage.

This last point is particularly important. If the broker receives less than £250 for arranging the mortgage, they don't have to tell you; otherwise you should see in writing the full amount. This is to ensure you are getting the right mortgage and not just one that pays the person who arranged it a large sales commission.

'CAT' standards

The government recently introduced CAT standards for mortgages. CAT stands for charges, access and terms, and to achieve the CAT standard, these must be fair and clearly explained. As the CML points out, a CAT standard mortgage is not necessarily better than a non-CAT one, but it may suit you if you are looking for a straightforward mortgage deal.

The different types of mortgage

Repayment mortgages

With a repayment mortgage every payment you make to the lender repays part of the actual money borrowed (the capital) and part of the interest on the loan. If you make all the necessary payments you can be sure that you will repay the mortgage by the agreed date.

This makes repayment mortgages the best option if you have a very cautious attitude to risk and you want the simplest arrangement.

Interest only

The alternative to a repayment mortgage is an interest-only loan where you make interest payments each month but the capital debt remains static. At the same time, you save through an investment vehicle to build up a large enough fund to repay the mortgage at the end of its term and, possibly, create a surplus lump sum for your own use. Unless you go for an endowment, you also need to take out sufficient life assurance to repay the loan if you or your partner dies before your fund has grown to the required level.

For details on how endowment, Isa and pension mortgages work, read Chapter 16, and also refer to chapters 11, 12 and 21 on these investments.

Your choice of interest rates

These days, it is rare for a new borrower not to be able to find some sort of special deal on the interest rate. Your financial adviser will be able to run through the complete range at the time you wish to take out the loan, but this section describes briefly your main options. Bear in mind, as always, that there is no such thing as a free lunch. Somewhere along the line you must pay for the special feature, which usually means committing yourself to a minimum number of years with that lender or facing a penalty if you want to switch to a different mortgage or repay a capital lump sum to reduce the outstanding debt.

Annual percentage rate

Before looking at the various options, it is helpful to understand how the interest rate is calculated and applied. There are many variations on this theme – for example, a lender might calculate and charge the interest on a daily, monthly, quarterly or even annual basis, all of which affect the annual rate charged.

To enable you to make meaningful comparisons between lenders' offers, the government introduced the concept of the 'annual percentage rate of change' or APR. This represents the total charge for credit and takes into account the added costs of the loan, such as the valuation fees and lender's conveyancing charges, which are not included in the nominal rate. The APR is based on the gross rate of interest, so for existing loans only it does not take account of mortgage interest relief at source (MIRAS), which was abolished for new mortgages after April 5, 2000.

One word of warning. The APR quoted for fixed-rate or discount schemes only applies to the offer period – it does not take into account the full variable rate which will kick in after the cheap rate has finished.

Variable rate

Lenders frequently change the interest rate for borrowers and savers and these increases and decreases are passed on to your monthly repayments. Where the institution has borrowers and savers – the building societies and banks, for example – they need to retain a margin between the two, as this represents their 'turn'. If they have to pay more to savers to keep a competitive edge, they will have to pass on this increase to mortgage customers. Other factors which influence mortgage rates include fluctuations in the Bank of England's base rate and, for the 'centralized' lenders, the cost of raising funds on the money markets.

Fixed rate

This type of mortgage is particularly attractive to borrowers who want the comfort of knowing what their liabilities are for several years in order to budget accurately. Typically lenders are prepared to fix for one or two years, sometimes up to five. When the fixed-rate period ends you would switch to the lender's variable rate or perhaps be offered the chance to fix again.

The factors that influence a decision to go for a fixed rate as a borrower are similar to the considerations facing a saver, but in reverse. If general interest rates rise, you will be protected from an increase in your repayments for the period covered. However, if interest rates fall, you will be locked into an uncompetitively high rate.

> The factors that influence a decision to go for a fixed rate as a borrower are similar to the considerations facing a saver, but in reverse.

As with savers who go for a fixed-rate bond, for example, fixed-rate borrowers must watch out for early redemption penalties. Quite often these are so high that you are forced to stay put because it is too expensive to get out, even when you take into account much better rates elsewhere.

Discounted rate

Most lenders offer a discount of 1 per cent or 2 per cent off their variable rate, usually for a period of one or two years. On top of this, a lender may provide a 'cashback', where a lump sum is paid to the borrower once the mortgage has been settled. This type of package can be very attractive if you want to keep payments down during the first few years, but if you are interested, make sure you are happy with the penalties for early redemption or for repaying part of your debt with a lump sum. In the latter case, you would forfeit the cashback and you would have to pay, typically, the difference between the discount and standard variable rate on the lump sum you use to reduce the mortgage. Under this system, the longer you stick with the lender, the worse the partial repayment penalty will be, until, that is, you are clear of the penalty period.

Cap and collar mortgages

Under a cap and collar mortgage, the lender sets an upper and lower limit on fluctuations in the interest rate. This means you know the worst in advance – the rate cannot exceed the upper limit. However, if interest rates fall below the 'collar', you will be stuck with an uncompetitive package, just as you would be with a fixed-rate mortgage. Penalties are likely to apply if you want to re-mortgage to take advantage of better rates elsewhere.

Mortgate-related insurance

Due to the substantial size of the loan and the value of the property, it is important to make sure you have the right type of insurance. In some cases this will be a compulsory requirement by the lender, although usually you can choose your own insurer so, as ever, do shop around or use an independent financial adviser to do so for you. It may seem easier at the time to go with the lender's choice, but this may prove an expensive mistake.

Buildings and contents insurance are essential, and both the CML and ABI guides offer some good advice for buyers. In this chapter, however, we limit the examination to the mortgage-related insurance that protects the lender if you default, and the personal insurances which either pay off the debt in the event of your death or help you maintain repayments in the event of long-term illness.

Mortgage indemnity

Financial institutions like to protect themselves if they lend you more than 75 per cent of the value of the property. The risk they face is that if you default they would need to repossess the house and sell it, probably for less than the purchase price, given they wouldn't want to keep an empty property on their books in order to wait for prices to rise. So, if you want a 'high loan to value' advance, lenders reckon they are justified in making you pay towards the mortgage indemnity insurance, which would reimburse them for some or all of the difference between the outstanding mortgage and the actual selling price.

> The important point to remember about the mortgage indemnity fee (it might also be called an additional security fee or high-percentage loan fee) is that it protects the lender, not you.

The important point to remember about the mortgage indemnity fee (it might also be called an additional security fee or high-percentage loan fee) is that it protects the lender, not you.

Life assurance

Life assurance is examined in detail in Chapter 2, but briefly, your life assurance should pay off all your outstanding liabilities. The mortgage is likely to be your main debt, but you should also factor in any other liabilities, whether they are debts (hire purchase agreements and other loans) or regular commitments such as school fees for your children.

With an endowment mortgage, the endowment plan combines both the savings and the life assurance element. If you prefer to save through an Isa, for example, you must buy the life assurance separately.

There are several types of life assurance, but the simplest and cheapest is likely to be level term assurance, which provides a lump sum if you die during the insured period, but nothing if you do not. This lump sum should, when invested, generate a replacement income, taking into account any company benefits such as dependants' pensions and lump sum death benefits. You should also consider family income benefit or some other type of life assurance to cover the partner who looks after the children.

Family income benefit could, for example, be used to pay for a live-in nanny, to enable the surviving spouse to continue to work.

Payment protection

This is a variation on critical illness and/or permanent health insurance (see Chapter 3). If you suffer a chronic illness or become disabled, this type of policy would cover the cost of the mortgage and any related costs – insurances for example. The critical illness element would provide a lump sum if you suffered a major illness.

You might also be offered a third type of policy, known as accident, sickness and unemployment (ASU) insurance. This covers your monthly mortgage payments if you become too ill to work or are unemployed. The accident and sickness element is like a short-term PHI policy. Unemployment insurance is available through a few specialist insurers but generally is very expensive, so ASU may be the only way to get it.

Following social security changes, if you are a new borrower, you now have to wait nine months before you can claim unemployment benefit to cover your mortgage – longer if you have savings of £8,000 or more. You can use ASU to insure the nine-month gap, and in some cases can cover yourself for up to two years.

However, experts warn you should treat this type of insurance as a way of buying some breathing space if you need to re-assess your finances in the light of illness or unemployment. It does not provide a long-term replacement income.

The same caveat applies to the limited versions of PHI and critical illness offered through a mortgage protection scheme. The main point to note here is that, while the lender is concerned to ensure you keep up your monthly repayments, in practice you will need a great deal more than this to cover all your monthly outgoings and your liabilities. This is particularly important if you are self-employed, and therefore not covered by an employer's group scheme at work.

In conclusion, our advice is to check what cover you have through an employer's scheme and any existing private insurance, and read Chapters 19 and 21 to find out how the different policies work and how to calculate the total level of income and capital you need to insure.

Read the small print

■ **Simplified acceptance for life assurance:** This is a short cut to buying the life assurance you need to cover your mortgage debt if you die. Buying life assurance can be time-consuming, and often involves completing a detailed questionnaire and attending a private medical. However, some providers will insure you without these requirements if you are under the age of 50 and need less than £70,000 of cover. To qualify, usually you must also provide satisfactory responses to three questions about whether you have visited your GP in the last few months, whether you are taking medication and whether you have had an HIV test, counselling or advice. You might also be asked if you have any dangerous pastimes – motor racing or hang-gliding, for example.

- **Free temporary life cover:** Once you exchange contracts you are legally bound to the mortgage, but your life cover may not take effect until completion. To avoid the potential complications that would arise if a borrower died in the period between exchange and completion, some companies provide free cover for up to three months from exchange.

- **Transfers from joint to single life:** Given that one marriage in three ends in divorce, it is important to check that your policy will not need to be cancelled if the house and investment have to change from joint to single ownership. This is particularly important where your life assurance and investment are combined through an endowment since policies stopped in the early years are usually very poor value. Rather than cancel the policy on divorce, some providers allow one of the partners to continue the premiums unchanged or they might alter the life assurance and premiums to reflect the new ownership.

- **Guaranteed insurability options:** These give you the flexibility to increase the level of life assurance if you move house, improve your home or if your family situation changes, for example on marriage or on the birth of a child. Some insurers will increase cover without a medical examination or detailed application form.

Summary

- Seek independent financial advice on both the choice of mortgage and the investment plan you use to repay the debt.
- Most mortgage institutions will lend up to three times your annual salary, twice your joint salary, or three times the main and once the second salary.
- Check the penalties which apply to any special offers such as a fixed rate or discount on the variable rate.
- Use the annual percentage rate (APR) to make comparisons between different lenders, but remember this will relate to the offer period if there is a discount or fixed rate.

- Make sure your life assurance and income protection plans cover all your liabilities and requirements, not just what you need to repay the mortgage.
- Check whether the life assurance covers you for the period between exchange and completion.

Glossary of terms

Cap and collar refers to interest rates which can vary between an upper and lower limit.

Discounted rates offer a reduction of, say, 1–2 per cent off the variable rate.

Fixed rate refers to interest payments which are fixed for a period of one to five years.

Interest-only mortgages require you to pay just the interest each month, and to save in a suitable plan (e.g. individual savings account) to repay the capital debt at maturity.

Mortgage indemnity insurance is an extra payment charged by the lender if the advance is more than 75 per cent of the purchase price.

Repayment mortgages: Here your monthly payments include interest and capital so that at the end of the mortgage term you have paid the entire debt.

Variable rate refers to repayments where the interest fluctuates in line with the lender's main rate.

Further information

Council of Mortgage Lenders (*www.cml.org.uk*): For a free guide *How to Buy a Home* or *How to Buy a Home in Scotland*, send a large stamped addressed envelope to the Council of Mortgage Lenders, BSA/CML Bookshop, 3 Savile Row, London W1X 1AF. The CML also publishes a free leaflet on taxation and the homebuyer.

Association of British Insurers: For free fact sheets on mortgage protection insurance, buildings and contents insurance, write to the Association of British Insurers, 51 Gresham Street, London EC2V 7HQ or visit the website at *www.abi.org.uk*.

Investing to repay your mortgage

Next to your pension, the investment you choose to repay your mortgage is likely to be your most valuable asset. Historically, the big mortgage lenders were biased towards endowments, partly because the life offices paid handsome sales commissions, and partly because until the early 1980s endowments were favoured by the taxation system which granted tax relief on life assurance premiums. This tax advantage has all but vanished, yet endowments still account for a large proportion of mortgage repayment methods.

In recent years, the more expensive and inflexible endowments have been the subject of fierce criticism. At present the Financial Services Authority is investigating complaints from many home owners who believe they were mis-sold an endowment and have lost out financially as a result. The FSA guide to making a complaint is available from 0800 917 3311. If the firm that sold the endowment has gone out of business or you can't trace it, contact the FSA Consumer Helpline on 0845 606 1234.

> The tax advantages of endowments have all but vanished, yet they still account for a large proportion of the mortgage repayment market.

The debate over the suitability of endowment mortgages, which came at a time of falling investment returns and rising mortgage rates, presented a powerful argument in favour of the traditional repayment mortgage where monthly payments cover the interest and also pay off the capital debt (see Chapter 15). Nevertheless, for many homeowners a good quality predominantly equity-based investment plan is likely to build up a fund

FINANCIAL SNAPSHOT

If you move house and already have an endowment, don't cancel it, but consider topping up your loan with an Isa or a repayment mortgage.

which will repay the mortgage at maturity, and which will prove to be more flexible than the repayment version.

Of course, you have to bear in mind the caveat that an interest-only loan backed by an investment plan offers no guarantee that you will be free of debt at the end of the mortgage period.

The most common investments recommended by advisers to repay mortgages are life assurance endowments and Individual savings accounts. In some cases personal pensions are also used, but here you must be very careful not to reduce your retirement fund to an inadequate level.

These investments are examined in detail in Chapters 11, 12 and 21 respectively. To avoid duplication, in this chapter we limit the discussion to comments on the suitability of each method.

You don't have to restrict your choice to these particular investments. Lenders increasingly are taking a more flexible attitude as to how you repay your mortgage. Depending on your income and other savings, some are prepared to offer a mortgage without insisting that you establish an investment plan specifically earmarked to repay the debt. This is ideal for sophisticated investors who want to retain total freedom over their portfolio and may ultimately use a combination of investments to pay back the loan.

One word of warning on flexibility, however. If you move house and need a bigger mortgage, don't cancel the endowment policy – it may be better to top up using some other method such as an Isa or repayment. If the performance of your endowment is dismal, then as a last resort it might be worth trying to sell it through the second-hand endowment market (see Further information below).

Finally, borrowers keen to clear their debt early should always check for any penalties. As we discussed in the last chapter, most of the special offers – the fixed-rate and discount mortgages – impose stiff penalties if you want to reduce your debt through additional capital payments or want to pay it off altogether.

Endowment mortgages

The main difference between endowments and other investments is that endowments combine life assurance with the savings plan. Where you use other investments to back a mortgage – an Isa, for example – you have to buy life assurance separately.

One of the big selling features of endowments in the 1970s and early 1980s was life assurance premium relief. This was abolished for new endowments taken out after March 1984 and ended for existing endowments on April 5, 2000.

In recent years endowments have faced serious criticism. Evidence of widespread 'churning' for extra sales commission in the 1980s, when investors were persuaded to cancel an existing policy and take out a new product, tarnished the endowment's reputation. Many policyholders still assume that the endowment guarantees to pay off the mortgage at maturity. In fact this was never guaranteed but it has taken a period of falling returns to bring this point home. Thousands of policyholders have had to increase monthly premiums to keep on target to repay the debt.

As with any investment, the size of the fund at maturity depends largely on three factors:

- the amount you pay to the financial institution
- the amount actually invested after charges and the cost of the life assurance are deducted
- the investment performance.

In response to criticism, several leading endowment companies have altered their product structure to offer better value and greater flexibility, in particular by improving their terms for investors who stop a policy early. However, there are still some pretty awful endowments around which combine poor performance with high charges and are so inflexible that once you are in it is very hard to get out again without losing a lot of money.

If you still think an endowment is the right sort of investment for you, consider these points:

- **Charges:** Past performance is an unreliable guide to the future, but when it comes to endowment premiums and charges we are dealing with known facts. Prior to January 1, 1995, providers did not have to tell you how much of your premiums disappeared in charges. Now the life offices must give all prospective clients a pre-sale 'key features' document that sets out the total deductions over the course of the investment period. Among other points this document shows you what the effect of the charges will be and what you are likely to get back if you pull out early. Clearly this information is of use only if the charges of different companies are compared. In some cases, the total bill for charges represents about one-third of the potential investment return. Ideally, you should only buy an endowment through an independent financial adviser who will check this is the most suitable investment to back your

> There are still some pretty awful endowments around which combine poor performance with high charges and are so inflexible that once you are in it is very hard to get out again without losing a lot of money.

mortgage and who will select the best company in terms of performance, charges and flexibility.

- **Cashing in early:** Unfortunately, the consequences of cashing in your endowment policy early remain dire with the majority of providers. Recent surveys indicated that over half of the unit-linked endowments and one-third of the 'with profits' plans provide no return after one year. Several provide no return after two years. If you cash in after ten years, almost one-third of the endowments do not even return your original premiums.

- **Beware low premiums:** When you shop around for a mortgage, bear in mind that a low premium does not necessarily represent good value but may simply be a gamble on high investment returns which, if they fail to materialize, will force the life office to increase your premiums or leave you to face a significant shortfall in the fund needed at maturity to pay off your mortgage.

- **Early repayment can damage your wealth:** If you decide to pay off your mortgage early and terminate your endowment in the few years before maturity, you may be in for a shock. For a 25-year endowment, the difference between the return at Year 24 and Year 25 can be as much as 20 per cent of the total payout in some cases.

Pep/Isa mortgages

In Chapter 12, we explained why individual savings accounts are more tax-efficient than endowments. You can also pay what you want, when you want, provided you stick to the overall Revenue annual limits.

> It's not a win-win situation with Isas. Where you gain on tax efficiency and flexibility you can lose out on the higher charges.

But it's not a win-win situation with Isas. Where you gain on tax efficiency and flexibility you can lose out on charges. Over the long term, it is the annual management charges that really bite and in many cases these are higher under an Isa than an endowment, with the exception of the index trackers.

Isa mortgages are similar to unit-linked endowment mortgages. However, instead of using an endowment plan to cover both the life assurance and savings required to pay off the debt, with an Isa mortgage, the Isa is used as the savings vehicle, and a separate life assurance policy is taken out to pay off the debt in the event of the death of one of the borrowers.

These points also apply to those who plan to use a Pep to repay their mortgage. Isas replaced Peps in 1999. Although you can no longer add to a Pep you can keep the funds built up to date in their tax-efficient Pep wrapper and make new contributions to an Isa (see Chapter 12).

Pension mortgages

The tax-free cash available at retirement from pension arrangements can also be used to repay a mortgage. As explained in Chapter 21, with a pension plan you get full tax relief on premiums and the fund grows free of tax. The pension itself is taxed as income.

In theory, then, a personal pension plan should make a very tax-efficient repayment vehicle, but there is an important caveat. If you fund your mortgage solely from this source you could leave yourself with a diminished fund at retirement with which to buy your annuity. Consequently, there is a real danger this would leave you with a low income in retirement.

Summary

- The investment you choose to repay your mortgage is likely to be your most valuable asset after the house itself and your pension fund.
- Lenders today are very flexible on which investment you use to back your mortgage, but the most popular choices are endowments and Isas.
- Some endowments offer poor value, but some provide a good combination of consistent long-term performance and low charges.
- Isas are more tax-efficient than endowments, but check the charges as these tend to be higher, particularly the annual management charge. This can undermine your return over the long term.
- Pension mortgages are very tax-efficient, but be careful not to deplete your fund to the point where you end up with a low income in retirement.
- Don't pay off your mortgage early without first checking any penalties under the investment plan and the mortgage itself.

Glossary of terms

Endowments combine life assurance and an investment to repay the mortgage. They can be inflexible.

Pensions can be a tax efficient way to repay a mortgage but most people need all their pension fund to provide a retirement income.

Peps/Isas are purely investments, so you have to buy separate life assurance. These are considered more tax efficient and flexible than endowments. Isas replaced Peps in 1999 but you can keep existing funds in the tax-efficient Pep wrapper.

Further information

For information about selling an endowment see page 102.

Home income plans

Home income plans offer elderly people who are 'house-rich, cash-poor' the opportunity to tap into the equity in their homes and use this to generate an extra income. These plans are particularly attractive because you don't have to sell up and move. You can take the money as a regular income or as a lump sum, depending on the scheme rules.

The plans sold in the late 1980s led many pensioners to make unwise investments and they were banned in 1990. But with increased longevity and cuts in state welfare provision, asset-rich, cash-poor pensioners are turning for financial assistance to a second generation of much more respectable equity-release plans.

> Following the bad publicity of the earlier plans, four companies – Allchurches Life, Carlyle Life, Home & Capital Trust and Stalwart Assurance – joined together in 1991 to form SHIP, the Safe Home Income Plans company.

Safe as houses?

Following the bad publicity of the earlier plans, four companies – Allchurches Life, Carlyle Life, Home & Capital Trust and Stalwart Assurance – joined together in 1991 to form SHIP, the Safe Home Income Plans company. Since then other companies have joined. The SHIP secretariat is based at the independent advisers and home income plan specialists

F I N A N C I A L   S N A P S H O T

In households where the owner is 65 or older, about 54 per cent are owner-occupiers without a mortgage.

Hinton & Wild. The code of practice offered by members of the organization is as follows:

- You have complete security of tenure and are guaranteed the right to live in the property for life, no matter what happens to interest rates and the stock market.
- You have freedom to move house without jeopardizing your financial situation.
- You will be guaranteed a cash sum or regular income; your money will not be sunk into uncertain investments.

How do they work?

There are two basic types of safe home income plans – those where a mortgage on the property is used to produce an income, and those which involve the sale of part or all of your property to produce an income or cash lump sum. In each case the loan is paid off when you die.

Mortgage annuities

Mortgage-based schemes have been much less popular since the 1999 Budget abolished mortgage interest tax relief at source (MIRAS). This type of plan allows you to re-mortgage part of the value of your house – usually up to £30,000. The lump sum is used to buy a 'purchased life annuity' from the lender, which in return guarantees an income for life. This pays the fixed rate of interest on the mortgage, and what's left is yours to spend how you wish. Until the 1999 Budget the mortgage interest was net of MIRAS at the concessionary rate of 23 per cent, but only loans taken out before April 1999 continue to qualify. This move has made 'reversion' plans more suitable in most cases.

Reversion plans

This is where you sell, rather than mortgage, part or all of your house. Reversion plans fall into two categories. With a **reversion annuity**, the purchase price is used to buy an annuity which operates in the same way as the mortgage annuity described above, although obviously there is no mortgage interest to pay so your income is higher. However, because you have sold rather than mortgaged, you will not gain from any rise in house prices on that portion of your property. The exception is the Stalwart reversion plan which links its annuity to its property fund, and therefore passes on some of the gains in property price rises in the form of increased income. If you are concerned about the downside risk, Stalwart will guarantee 50 per cent of your annuity rate.

Under the **cash option** you sell part or all of your home in return for a lump sum which is tax-free provided the house is your main residence. You continue to live there, rent free, until you die. You can, if you wish, use the money to buy an annuity, but this is not obligatory.

According to SHIP, the minimum age for reversion plans is 65 to 70. The minimum sale is usually between 40 per cent and 50 per cent of the value of the property, and with most companies you can sell up to 100 per cent. SHIP says that for homes priced over £70,000, the benefits under a reversion plan often are appreciably higher than the mortgage plans.

How to decide

Your choice of plan will depend partly on your age and your view on whether house prices are likely to rise over the period of the loan. But there are other factors involved. For example, you should consider how the additional income will affect your tax position and the possible loss of means-tested social security benefits. In particular, care is needed if you receive income support or council tax benefits, as these may be reduced or lost altogether. Clearly the home income plan benefits must more than compensate for this loss.

You should also check how an equity release scheme would affect your inheritance tax position, and you may wish to discuss your plans with your family, since it will reduce your estate. Moreover, before entering into an agreement, ask what would happen if you have to leave your house, perhaps to move into sheltered accommodation or a nursing home.

Finally, do consider all the costs involved, for example the survey, legal fees and administrative charges. Some plan providers make a contribution, but amounts vary.

Summary

- Home income plans may be suitable if you need to boost your income and have no other assets to draw on except the equity tied up in your home.
- You can sell all or part of an interest in your home and use the money to buy an annuity. The debt is repaid when you die and the house is sold.

- Make sure you fully understand the terms of the plan and seek legal advice before proceeding.
- Find out how the plan will affect your income tax position and whether there are implications for inheritance tax.

Glossary of terms

Cash reversion plans allow you to sell part or all of your home in return for a lump sum. You continue to live there, rent free, until you die. You can use the money to buy an annuity but this is not obligatory.

Mortgage annuities allow you to re-mortgage part of the value of your house – usually up to £30,000. The lump sum is used to buy a **purchased life annuity** which pays the interest on the mortgage and provides an income. Since April 1999 tax relief has not been available on interest payments on new loans.

Reversion annuities allow you to sell part of the interest in your house and use the proceeds to buy an annuity to provide the income.

Further information

Safe Home Income Plans: 01242 539494 or *www.ship-ltd.co.uk*.

Pensions

State pensions

The government's new 'stakeholder' pension schemes should extend low-cost private provision to those not already in a company scheme. However, you should still make the most of your state benefits.

Pension forecasts

The calculation of the state pension is ridiculously complicated. If, like most people, you feel there must be more to life than wading through a morass of documents, ask your local Department of Social Security for a pension forecast (form BR19). This should provide a fairly intelligible explanation of your entitlement. You can get a pension forecast provided you have more than four months to go to pensionable age.

If you just want to find out what your additional pension will be, ask for leaflet NP 38. This type of forecast should help you decide whether or not to contract out of the additional pension scheme, for example if you want to take out a personal pension plan.

> If you want to find out what your pension is worth, and you feel there must be more to life than wading through obscure documents, ask your local Department of Social Security for a pension forecast (form BR19).

FINANCIAL SNAPSHOT

People mistakenly believe the National Insurance Fund is storing up assets to pay their pension. Well, there isn't a fund. Social security is based on the 'pay-as-you-go' system, so no sooner have you paid in your NI contributions than the DSS uses them to pay someone else's benefits.

Each forecast takes between three and six weeks to process, longer if you are widowed or divorced, where the assessment will be more complicated.

How the state pension works

The pension has two elements – a basic flat-rate pension, known as the old age pension, and a pension which is linked to the level of your earnings, known as the 'additional pension' or 'Serps' (state earnings-related pension scheme), which is being replaced by a new flat-rate scheme shortly. Eligibility to both pensions is built up through the compulsory payment of National Insurance (NI) contributions on part of your earnings. The National Insurance system is explained briefly below.

The maximum single person's basic state pension for the 2001–2002 tax year is £72.50 per week, while the maximum additional or Serps pension is just over £130 per week. State pensions rise each year in line with retail prices, are taxed as earned income and should be included in the end-of-year tax return.

The official pension age – 65 for men and 60 for women – is the minimum age at which men and women can claim a state pension in the UK. By the year 2020, the UK will have a common pension age of 65 for both men and women. This move to equal pension ages will result in a rather complex phasing period. Basically, women born after April 1955 will have to wait until age 65 to claim. Older women should check with the Department of Social Security to find out their proposed retirement date. The phasing period will last ten years between 2010 and 2020.

Don't fall into the trap of thinking that you will automatically receive the full rate of pension, even if you have worked for 40 years before retiring. The state pension system works relatively smoothly if you are employed from age 16 up to state pension age. However, the career pattern of many people involves periods in self-employment, periods spent not working in order to raise a family, periods in and out of company pension schemes, and a whole host of variables.

National Insurance and the state pension

State pensions come under the general heading of 'social security benefits' which also include benefits paid to people who are sick, disabled, out of work, or on a low income. Most of these benefits are paid for out of the National Insurance Fund, which is built up from National Insurance contributions levied on earnings and paid by employers, employees and the self-employed. Purists might disagree, but essentially NI contributions can be regarded as another form of direct taxation.

National Insurance for employees is levied on what are known as 'band earnings', that is earnings between lower and upper limits (known as the lower earnings limit or LEL and the upper earnings limit or UEL). These are £87 and £575 per week for the 2001–2002 tax year. The contributions are deducted automatically from an employee's pay packet while the self-employed pay a flat-rate contribution each month to the Department of Social Security and an earnings-related supplement which is assessed annually through the tax return.

The married woman's stamp

Women's state pensions are particularly complicated due to a two-tier National Insurance contribution system which still allows some older women (those who were married or widowed before April 5, 1977) to pay a reduced rate, known as the 'married woman's stamp'. The married woman's stamp originally was popular because it meant a much lower deduction from the weekly or monthly pay cheque. But if you pay this rate, you do not build up a right to a state pension in your own name. Instead you have to claim through your spouse's NI contribution record, and claim a Category B state pension which is worth about 60 per cent of the full rate.

The basic 'old age' pension

To get the full weekly rate of the basic pension, currently worth £72.50, you must have 'qualifying years' for about 90 per cent of your working life. Broadly speaking, that is years in which you paid the full rate of National Insurance contributions for the complete period. In some cases you will be treated as though you had received qualifying earnings if you are eligible for certain benefits, for example Home Responsibilities Protection, invalid care allowance, unemployment benefit and sickness benefit, among others.

To get the minimum basic pension payable (25 per cent of the full rate), you normally need a minimum of ten qualifying years.

It is not possible to claim the state pension before you reach official pension age, but it is possible to defer claiming for up to five years and earn increments.

> It is not possible to claim the state pension before you reach official pension age, but it is possible to defer claiming for up to five years and earn increments.

Married couple's pension

The combination of the single person's pension and the spouse's pension (Category B – £43.40) form what is generally known as the married couple's state pension, which is worth £115.90 for the 2001–2002 tax year.

If a woman qualifies for a single person's (Category A) state pension in her own right but it is worth less than the Category B pension, when her husband reaches age 65 or retires to claim his pension she will receive a composite pension worth a maximum of the full Category B rate.

Under the current system the Category B pension, sometimes referred to as a 'dependency increase', is most frequently paid to the husband on behalf of his 'dependent' wife. Government proposals are likely to equalize the conditions for eligibility so that an older woman can claim a Category B pension for her husband, provided he does not have earnings or other pensions worth more than the value of the dependency pension.

The minimum income guarantee (MIG)

The government offers a range of benefits to provide extra support to very low income pensioners. In particular the Minimum Income Guarantee, paid through Income Support, tops up the basic pension to £92.15 (single person) and £140.55 (married couple) if you qualify.

The basic pension and your company scheme

'Integrated' company schemes are very common. Under this system, the level of pension promised by the company scheme takes into account the basic state pension. Effectively, this means that the employer does not provide any pension for earnings up to the lower earnings limit (£87 per week in 2001–2002) or a multiple of this. Low earners and those who do not qualify for a state pension in their own right can suffer as a result.

Additional pension ('Serps')

The second tier of the state pension is the element which is linked to part of your earnings, known as 'additional pension' or 'Serps' (state earnings-related pension scheme). This pension, worth just over £130 for the 2001–2002 tax year, is paid at the same time as the basic pension, that is at age 65 for men and between age 60 and 65 for women, depending on when they retire.

If you are an employee and you are not contracted out of Serps, either through a company pension scheme or an appropriate personal pension plan, automatically you will be a member and pay for the pension through your National Insurance contributions.

Unlike the basic state pension, where the minimum qualifying contribution period is about ten years to get any benefit at all, a right to Serps builds up from day one. The value of the pension depends on the level of your earnings and the contribution period. It will also depend on when you reach pension age, because the government has reduced Serps for those who retire after April 5, 1999. This, combined with the planned phased increase in women's pension age from 60 to 65, which kicks off in 2010, makes the calculation of the additional pension an extremely complicated exercise.

How Serps is calculated

Your Serps pension will be worth 25 per cent of your National Insurance band earnings averaged over the period 1978/79 and April 6, 1999. For benefits built up after this date, the formula is reduced over a ten-year period from 25 per cent to 20 per cent of band earnings averaged over your entire working life.

If you are a member of a company pension scheme which is contracted out of Serps, or if you have an 'appropriate' personal pension, your additional pension is replaced by the private scheme or plan.

Changes to Serps

From 2002 the government will introduce changes that will provide a more generous flat rate benefit but only to low earners, certain carers and people with a long-term illness or disability. This will be called the State Second Pension.

'Inherited' Serps

From October 6, 2002, a new rule comes into force which will reduce the maximum amount of Serps that a widow or widower may inherit from their husband or wife, from 100 per cent to 50 per cent. Nobody who is widowed before October 6, 2002 will be affected by the new rule. Moreover, if your husband or wife is due to reach retirement age before this date, you will receive up to 100 per cent of their Serps when they die.

Appeals

Given the complexity of the state pension system it is not surprising that from time to time the DSS makes a mistake in the calculation of benefits. If you claim a social security benefit – whether it is your pension or some other form of payment – and you are unhappy about the decision made by the adjudication officer or adjudicating medical authority, you can request a review or make an appeal. However, first you should read leaflet NI 260 *A Guide to Reviews and Appeals* to make sure you understand the rules.

Summary

- To find out what your state pension is worth, ask your local DSS for a pension forecast.
- Don't assume you will receive a full pension automatically. The qualifying rules are very complex and you usually have to have worked all your life to get the maximum benefit.
- You can defer the date when you take your pension, but you cannot draw it early.
- If you think the DSS has miscalculated your pension you have the right to appeal.

Glossary of terms

Band earnings are the earnings between £87 and £575 per week for the 2001–2002 tax year, on which National Insurance is levied.

Contracted out refers to employees who have replaced their Serps pension either through a company scheme or a personal pension.

Inherited Serps: 50 per cent of your spouse's Serps will be paid to you if he/she dies after October 2002 but did not reach state retirement age before that date.

The married woman's stamp is a reduced rate of National Insurance contribution which can be paid by women who were married or widowed before April 1977.

National Insurance is a form of taxation levied on band earnings (see above).

Qualifying year: Your NI contributions count towards your state pension only if you pay for a complete year.

Serps: The state earnings-related pension scheme, which is based on National Insurance band earnings.

State Second Pension: A replacement for Serps for lower earners.

Further information

The Department of Social Security (DSS) publishes several guides to National Insurance and social security benefits which are available, free of charge, from local DSS offices or DSS Pensions, Freepost BS5555/1 Bristol BS99 1BL, phone 0845 7313233, *www.pensionguide.gov.uk*. Some leaflets are also available from post offices, libraries and Citizens Advice Bureaux (*www.nacab.org.uk*).

For details about The Minimum Income Guarantee, phone 0800 028 1111.

chapter nineteen

Company pension schemes

For most employees membership of the company pension scheme represents the most important benefit after the salary itself. But don't assume just because there *is* a company scheme that it is automatically going to see you right in retirement. Scheme benefits vary considerably, and you may need to top up your pension if your employer is less than generous.

Company schemes are very tax-efficient. The employer's contributions are tax deductible, the employee's contributions are paid free of basic and higher rate tax, the pension fund builds up virtually tax-free, and a significant chunk of the final benefits can be taken as tax-free cash at retirement. The pension, whether drawn from a company scheme or from a life office in the form of an annuity, is subject to your top rate of income tax.

> With a money purchase scheme the investment risk falls fairly and squarely on you, the scheme member. There are no guarantees.

There are two main types of occupational schemes: 'final salary', also known as 'defined benefit', and 'money purchase', also known as 'defined contribution'. With a final salary scheme, the employer bears the investment risk and backs the pension guarantees. With a money purchase scheme, the investment risk falls fairly and squarely on your shoulders as the scheme member and there are no guarantees.

FINANCIAL SNAPSHOT

Since 1988, employers have not been able to make membership of the scheme a condition of employment.

Stakeholder schemes

These new, government-backed personal pension schemes are covered in Chapter 21. They represent a low-cost private pension for employees who do not have access to a traditional company scheme, and they are likely to be cheaper than most personal pensions.

If you earn less than £30,000 you may pay into a personal pension as well as your company scheme.

Final salary schemes

Final salary or defined benefit (DB) schemes, still the most prevalent among employers in the UK, base the pension calculation on the number of years of service and your salary at or near retirement. A typical scheme guarantees to provide a pension that builds up at the rate of 1/60 of your final salary for each year of service up to an Inland Revenue maximum of 40/60 – that is, two-thirds final salary at retirement (restricted for some higher earners – see below).

How much do you contribute?

Employees can contribute up to 15 per cent of gross pay to an occupational scheme, although the most common rate is about 5 per cent. 'Pay' in this context is defined as basic salary plus, in some cases, benefits such as overtime, bonuses, and the taxable value of fringe benefits. If overtime or sales commission form a significant proportion of your gross earnings and this is not taken into account in your pensionable pay you could consider top-up provision through additional voluntary contributions (see Chapter 20).

The pension itself may be based on your average salary during the last three years before retirement or possibly your average salary during the period of scheme membership. A minority of schemes base it on the period of maximum earnings, which is ideal if you are in a job where earnings peak mid-career rather than towards the end of your working life.

Contributions and benefits for higher earners

Over the past five years the Revenue has restricted the pensions of certain high earners. In particular, some employees are subject to a cap of £95,400, for the 2001–2002 tax year, on which contributions and the final pension can be based. The cap applies to members of final salary schemes set up after the 1989 budget and members who joined any final salary scheme after June 1, 1989. For these employees the maximum contributions for the 2001–2002 tax year are limited to £14,310 (15 per cent of £95,400), while the maximum pension will be about £63,600 (two-thirds of the cap).

Unapproved schemes

There are two main types of pension to cater for earnings above the cap. 'Funded unapproved retirement benefit schemes' (furbs) are company schemes that are recognized by the Revenue, but are 'unapproved' for tax purposes. Under a furbs, the employer sets aside contributions to build up a pension fund for the employee's earnings in excess of the cap. Furbs usually operate on a money purchase basis. The furbs member will remain in the main company scheme and receive benefits in the usual way up to the level of the cap.

The fact that the furbs has an identifiable fund, written under trust for the employee, makes it the most secure arrangement for individuals affected by the earnings cap.

Under a furbs, the employee is taxed on the employer's contributions which are classed as a benefit in kind, rather like membership of the company's private medical scheme. However, the employer can treat these contributions as a trading expense for corporation tax purposes. Also, there is no employer's National Insurance contribution on these payments. The furbs fund is subject to income and capital gains tax.

Where the fund is used to buy an annuity, the income is subject to tax. However, the entire benefit can be taken as a tax-free lump sum on retirement – a far more attractive option and the most common choice. The death-in-service lump sum benefits can be paid under discretionary trust and therefore should be free of inheritance tax.

> The fact that the furbs has an identifiable fund, written under trust for the employee, makes it the most secure arrangement for individuals affected by the earnings cap.

An alternative option under Inland Revenue rules is the unfunded unapproved retirement benefit scheme. In these arrangements your employer does not pay any contributions and there is no fund earmarked for the employee. Instead the pension benefits are paid out of company funds when the employee retires. When this happens the employer receives an allowance against corporation tax.

With this arrangement there is no tax liability until you receive the benefits but when that happens all lump sums and pensions are taxed as earned income. Where the employer decides to buy an annuity for the employee, the purchase price will be taxed as well as the resulting regular income. Death benefits, as with the furbs, should be free of inheritance tax if paid under a discretionary trust.

Topping up your company pension

By law every scheme, with a few minor exceptions, must provide an additional voluntary contribution (AVC) scheme which allows members to top up their company scheme benefits. In practice very few people end up with the maximum permitted pension so most will benefit from AVCs. Since 1987, employees also have been able to contribute to individual top-up plans known as free standing AVCs (FSAVCs), which are sold by insurance companies and other financial institutions. However, in most cases FSAVCs will be much more expensive than the in-house AVC scheme, while AVCs themselves may soon become a second-best alternative to stakeholder schemes, which can also be used by many employees to top up a company pension. These options are discussed in Chapter 20.

Transfers

This is one of the most complex pension issues. If you change jobs after two years' membership in a scheme you cannot claim a refund of contributions but instead have three main options.

■ You can leave your pension where it is. This is known as a preserved or 'deferred' pension since your right to a pension from that company scheme is put off or deferred until you reach pension age. By law the value of a deferred pension must increase in line with the retail price index up to a cap of 5 per cent. This is known as limited price indexation or LPI.

■ You can transfer the benefits to the new company scheme. This has the advantage of keeping all your benefits under one roof, but for various reasons you may not receive the same number of 'years' in the new scheme as you had built up in the old scheme.

However, despite the vagaries of deferred pensions and inter-company pension transfers, usually these two are the best options.

■ The other alternative is to transfer your benefits to an insurance product, either a personal pension or a 'buy-out' bond. This transaction will incur costs and the plans do not offer the guarantees associated with a final salary company scheme pension. Transfer options should always be considered with the help of an independent pensions adviser.

Integration

About 50 per cent of company schemes reduce the pension by 'integrating' with the basic state pension. The idea behind this is to provide a maximum two-thirds final salary pension including the state benefit. Of course it also cuts company pension costs. Where a scheme is integrated, no pension is paid for the first slice of salary up to the NI lower earnings limit (see page 152). No employee or employer pension contributions are levied on this amount either.

Contracting out of Serps

Most final salary schemes are contracted out of the state earnings-related pension scheme, and as a result the employer and employees pay a reduced rate of National Insurance contribution, with the balance invested in the company pension fund. Where the scheme is not contracted out, the employee would receive the Serps pension and the company pension on top of this.

Tax-free cash

The maximum tax-free cash you can take from your company pension scheme is one and a half times your final salary after 40 years' service. This is limited in the case of some higher earners (see page 158). If you take the tax-free cash – and almost everyone does – your pension will be reduced (the system is slightly different in public sector schemes).

Pension increases

Company schemes typically increase pensions by 3–5 per cent each year. However, you need to check which increases are guaranteed, and which are 'discretionary' (a voluntary payment on the part of the trustees when the fund has a surplus). Public sector pensions automatically increase in line with the full retail price index.

> Most final salary schemes provide other important family protection benefits in addition to the pension itself, for example, death-in-service benefits worth up to four times annual salary, widow's and dependent children's pensions and similar death in retirement benefits.

HOW DOES YOUR SCHEME RATE?

If you want to check how your company pension scheme rates, consult your scheme booklet and compare the benefits listed with our ideal scheme.

Retirement pension: Paid from age 65 (age 60 would be a real bonus), based on service and final earnings.

Accrual rate (that is, the rate at which the pension builds up): One-sixtieth of final pay for each year of service.

Pensionable earnings: All earnings (apart from overtime or similar bonuses paid only during earlier years of employment).

Final pay calculation: The higher of either total earnings in the year prior to retirement or average annual earnings over any three-year period ending within ten years of retirement, uprated in line with the retail price index.

Pensionable service: Total service including maternity leave and certain temporary absences.

Lump sum on retirement: Revenue maximum (that is, the maximum amount of pension that can be converted to tax-free cash – normally one and a half times final remuneration after 40 years, possibly limited by the earnings cap).

Pension increases: Linked to the retail price index.

Ill-health pension: Equivalent to the amount the employee would have received had they remained in service until normal retirement age, at their current rate of pay.

Death in service benefits: This should include a dependent adult's pension of four-ninths the member's total earnings at death plus pensions for dependent children. Also a lump sum of four times annual earnings.

Death in retirement benefits: This should include a pension worth two-thirds of the member's pension to be paid to a nominated adult dependant plus a pension for any dependent children under age 18.

Scheme leaver benefits: The whole of the preserved pension should be increased in line with the RPI up to retirement.

Source: Based on Union Pension Services' *Pension Scheme Profiles*

Family protection benefits

Most final salary schemes provide other important family protection benefits in addition to the pension itself, for example death in service benefits worth up to four times annual salary, widow's and dependent children's pensions and similar death in retirement benefits. Disability pensions and private medical insurance are also common features of the overall benefits package.

However, if you are not married to your partner, check whether they are still entitled to the benefits.

Stakeholder 'added extras'

A stakeholder pension is not the only product you will be offered from April 2001 via your employer. Most of the stakeholder providers are insurance companies and will be keen to sell you protection products such as life assurance, disability insurance, critical illness insurance (which pays a lump sum on diagnosis of a serious condition) and private medical insurance (PMI). Protection insurances are discussed in Section 2.

Selling financial products in the workplace – known as worksite marketing – is not new, but with the advent of stakeholder schemes it is expected to become far more prevalent. Products sold this way are known as 'voluntary benefits'. This means that although they are made available through your employer, the decision to buy is entirely up to you and the employer does not contribute. What your employer should be able to offer, however, is a discount due to the company's bulk negotiating and purchasing power. A well-negotiated voluntary benefits package should offer products at wholesale rates that are typically 25–30 per cent cheaper than you could find elsewhere.

The important point to bear in mind is that employers and insurance companies are not obliged to offer fair terms and low prices on anything other than the stakeholder scheme. Now stakeholder pension schemes are available, providers will have an excellent opportunity to cross-sell their other insurance and investment products to members of these schemes. Just because the stakeholder scheme is low cost, do not assume other products will offer equally good value.

While the product providers themselves must be authorized under the Financial Services Act, there are no rules that require your employer to screen the companies it welcomes into the workplace or allows to advertise on its intranet or benefits notice board. Moreover, while the stakeholder scheme is heavily regulated, critical illness and disability insurance (also known as permanent health insurance or PHI) are not covered by the

Financial Services Authority, nor are they regulated by the General Insurance Standards Council (GISC). The reality is that these products represent a gap in the regulatory floorboards. Caveat emptor still applies, therefore, to anything your employer may offer.

One of the most important products likely to be made available alongside the stakeholder scheme is 'waiver of premium'. If you become incapacitated or too ill to work, this insurance policy will continue payment of your pension premiums until your selected retirement date. Under personal pensions the cost typically adds 2.5–3 per cent to each premium but research suggests that stakeholder providers will charge a minimum of £5 per premium. This will be disproportionately high for those paying low contributions.

The range of non-pension voluntary benefits on offer will depend on the individual employer and is not necessarily limited to insurance products but could include anything from electrical goods to cheap holidays (see below).

How then can you decide whether the price and terms are worthwhile? Well, the first thing to do is ask how your employer negotiated the deals. Ideally the company will be using a fee-based benefits consultant, who will be able to search the market for the best prices and terms. Clearly you can make direct comparisons on price to find out if the voluntary benefit represents good value, but price isn't everything. Naturally the cost of the benefit is important but while advisers or employers should look for a competitive premium or price, they should not necessarily choose the cheapest. Equally important is the standard of service.

> Naturally the cost of the benefit is important but while advisers or employers should look for a competitive premium or price, they should not necessarily choose the cheapest. Equally important is the standard of service.

The Benefits Alliance – one of the biggest networks of employers who offer voluntary benefits – does not make any money from the deals it negotiates. This is an important point. Less scrupulous employers could take substantial commissions from sales of voluntary benefits where they negotiate them directly. Alternatively, if your employer uses an adviser who is remunerated by sales commission, this will also reduce the value of your benefit terms or increase the price. The Benefits Alliance requests that any commission the providers would usually pay is redirected into the deal to enhance the terms for the employees.

Finally, a word on tax. Generally speaking (and with the exception of pensions, critical illness and life assurance), where your employer pays for a benefit on your behalf, you may be liable to tax and/or National Insurance on the value of that benefit. With voluntary benefits your employer does not make any financial contribution. This means there are no taxation or NI considerations, although, of course, you are paying for the benefit out of taxed income.

What's on offer?

Voluntary benefits can include any or all of the following:

- annual travel insurance
- electrical goods
- health insurance, for example dental, eye care, lump sums for critical illness
- financial products, for example loans, mortgages, and saving schemes
- personal car purchase (new and second hand)
- gas and electricity supplies
- package holidays
- property conveyancing
- retail vouchers
- will writing
- plumbing insurance
- leisure activities.

Source: Based on the package negotiated by the Benefits Alliance.

What should your employer check?

Unlike a stakeholder pension scheme, your employer is under no obligation to screen products made available to you at work. Before buying in the workplace, find out how your employer has selected the products and services. For example:

- Is the price competitive? What is the discount compared with making the purchase as an individual?
- Has your employer checked standards of service?
- Are the terms and conditions fair?
- Are there any enhancements in addition to the standard product?
- How does the provider's track record compare with that of competitors? For example, how long has it been established, is it a market leader?

■ Does the process involve a sales commission to an intermediary or to the employer itself?

Your employer or the company's adviser should monitor each benefit on an annual basis to ensure the competitive price and quality of service are maintained.

Money purchase company schemes

Money purchase or defined contribution (DC) schemes can be attractive because you have an identifiable pot of money which you should be able to take from job to job. Contributions are invested to build up a fund which, at retirement, is used to buy an annuity from an insurance company. An annuity pays an income for life in return for a lump sum.

The most important point to bear in mind with money purchase is that the level of income your fund buys is not guaranteed, but will depend on four factors:

■ how much you and your employer contribute

■ the investment performance of the fund

■ the level of charges deducted from your fund by the pension company

■ annuity 'rates' – that is, the level of income your fund will buy at the time you retire.

How does your money purchase scheme rate?

Use the following checklist to find out whether your employer's money purchase scheme is well designed. Ideally it should:

■ aim (but it cannot guarantee) to match the pension and risk benefits equivalent to your old final salary scheme

■ invest minimum employer and employee total contributions of 6–15 per cent of annual salary, depending on age (the older you are, the more you need to pay in – see Table 19.1 on page 168).

■ delegate the investment management to a major institutional fund manager which has a proven track record in the pensions market

■ incur modest administration and investment charges which are shown to be among the most competitive for group schemes

■ impose no financial penalties if you leave the scheme when you change jobs, you reduce contributions, or you want to retire early.

If you don't want to make the investment decisions, your scheme should also offer a 'working life strategy'. This is a managed fund which provides you with the long-term growth potential of equities in the early years but protects your capital as you approach retirement by automatically phasing a switch from equities into cash and bonds.

Some employers are introducing money purchase schemes and asking members to switch from the old final salary scheme. If you are offered a choice between staying in your employer's old final salary scheme and joining the new money purchase scheme, you need practical advice from someone who fully understands how both schemes work. In particular, check that there are no material changes to the level of life assurance offered – typically three times your annual salary.

Contributions

Some money purchase schemes follow the same maximum contribution and benefit rules as final salary schemes. However, most new schemes are set up as group personal pensions (GPPs). Under a GPP, your individual personal pension plan can be used to contract out of Serps and to invest additional regular or single premiums to boost the pension provided by the NI rebate.

Under the new stakeholder tax regime, you can pay up to £3,600 per annum to any personal pension irrespective of earnings and even if you have no paid employment (see Chapter 21). If you want to pay more than this you must stick to a certain percentage of earnings based on age.

Personal pension contribution limits start at 17.5 per cent of 'net relevant earnings' (equivalent in this context to pensionable pay) for employees up to age 35, and rising in stages to 40 per cent for employees aged 61 and over. Employer contributions must be included in these limits, but there is no obligation for employers to pay anything other than the redirected NI contributions.

The contribution level is the litmus test of a good GPP. Table 19.1 gives you an idea of what you would need to contribute to achieve a pension similar in value to those offered by final salary schemes. The table (based on a real example provided by employee benefits consultants Godwins) shows the total contributions for a scheme designed to achieve broadly the same benefits as a final salary scheme where the pension builds up at a rate of 1/60 of final salary a year, allows for 3 per cent annual increases to the pension and provides a spouse's pension. Death in service benefits of four times salary are included, but in this case disability insurance is paid by the employer – otherwise the contributions necessary would be higher.

Table 19.1 Combined employee and employer contributions required to match a typical final salary scheme

Age	Total contribution (half paid by employer) % pa
16–24	6
25–29	7
30–34	8
35–39	9
40–44	10
45–49	11.5
50–54	13.5
55–59	15.5
60+	16.5

Source: Godwins

Family protection benefits

Death and disability benefits under money purchase schemes can be minimal so it is important to check what your employer provides here. If you are not happy with the level of cover offered, top up your family protection insurance through additional life assurance and disability or income replacement insurance. Private medical cover could also be considered.

> Flexibility is supposed to be one of the main attractions of money purchase pensions since the employee has an easily identifiable and apparently portable pot of money.

Flexibility and portability

Flexibility is supposed to be one of the main attractions of money purchase pensions since the employee has an easily identifiable and apparently portable pot of money. The important point to check here is what happens to your pot if you leave the scheme when you change jobs.

Special schemes for executives

Senior executives often belong to a fast-stream version of the main company pension scheme which builds up the pension more quickly and provides better benefits all round. But executives and directors can also be provided for through an entirely separate insurance arrangement known as an executive pension plan, or EPP. EPPs, although providing a pension linked to final salary, are occupational money purchase schemes designed for individuals or small groups of senior executives and directors.

In the past, EPPs have been popular, but today most advisers reckon that personal pensions, and particularly self-invested personal pensions (see Chapter 21), offer a package that is just as good and far simpler. Nevertheless, there are still some people for whom the EPP offers greater flexibility on contributions and possibly better and/or more flexible benefits, particularly as you can use an EPP in conjunction with the main company scheme (this is usually not possible with a personal pension).

So, for example, you could use an EPP to make contributions based on overtime and bonuses and then take the benefits from the plan as part of your early retirement income. You could start to draw benefits from your main company scheme at a later date. However, unlike SIPPs discussed in Chapter 21, you cannot usually separate the administration and investment under an EPP and this inflexibility could cost you dear in terms of sales commission payments to advisers and the life office charges.

Small company schemes

Small self-administered schemes (SSASs) come from the same stable as executive pension plans. These schemes are suitable for up to 12 members. Membership is usually restricted to the directors of the company because the fund can be used to invest in the business, for example to buy new premises. All investments must be at arm's length – so, in the case of a property purchase, the company would have to pay the scheme a commercial rate of rent.

SSASs are complicated and require expert advice.

Pensions and divorce

For most married couples, the husband's company pension is the most valuable asset after the family home. Over one-third of marriages in the UK end in divorce, but until 1996 there was no legal obligation to split the main breadwinner's (usually the husband's) pension fairly. Instead, in England and Wales, pension rights were dealt with at the discretion of the courts. In contrast, the law in Scotland is clear. Under the Family Law

(Scotland) Act 1985 'matrimonial property' specifically includes the proportion of pension and insurance rights accumulated during marriage, and in most cases these must be divided equally between the partners.

The law in England and Wales has changed in two distinct phases. Until December 2000 the courts could 'earmark' the spouse's share of the pension and this will be paid out at retirement, although if the spouse remarries, the earmarked pension, which is classed as deferred mainte-nance, reverts to the scheme member. After December 1, 2000, the court is able to demand an immediate split of the funds, so the lower-earning spouse can invest their share of the pension in a personal pension fund.

This whole area is very complex and you should seek professional advice on the calculation of your pension rights, particularly if you or your spouse have built up a substantial pension.

Summary

- In most cases it is in your interests to join the company scheme to take advantage of the employer's contributions.

- Higher earners may find the salary on which benefits and contributions are based is capped.

- If necessary, top up your scheme benefits with additional voluntary contributions or through a personal pension (see Chapter 20).

- Transfer of pension rights is a notoriously complicated exercise. Seek expert independent advice.

- Make sure your money purchase pension does not impose penalties if you stop or reduce contributions.

- There are special schemes for executives and directors: executive pension plans (EPPs) and small self-administered schemes (SSASs). These can be very tax-efficient, but they are complex – again seek expert independent advice.

- The same goes for divorce. Make sure your solicitor assesses the value of your spouse's pension and takes this into account in the financial settlement.

- Seek legal advice or help from the union if your company is changing hands and your pension scheme is affected.

Glossary of terms

Accrual rate: The rate at which your company pension builds up each year.

AVCs: additional voluntary contributions (AVCs) and free-standing AVCs allow you to top up your company pension in a tax-free fund.

Earnings cap restricts to £95,400 (in 2001–2002) the salary on which certain employees' pensions and contributions are based.

Final salary (defined benefit) schemes usually base the pension on your salary at or near retirement.

Funded unapproved retirement benefit scheme (furbs): An unapproved pension scheme used to cover earnings above the cap. **Unfunded unapproved retirement benefit schemes** are also for capped employees, but the tax treatment is less favourable.

Money purchase (defined contribution) schemes build up a fund which is used at retirement to buy an annuity. This pays an income for life.

Further information

The National Association of Pension Funds publishes a series of leaflets on company schemes and related issues. Many of these will be available free of charge from your pensions manager, but if not look at the website at *www.napf.co.uk* or write to the Association for a guide to its publications: The NAPF, 12–18 Grosvenor Gardens, London SW1W 0DH. Tel: 020 7730 0585. Fax: 0207 730 2595.

   The Department of Social Security also provides guides about occupational schemes (*www.dss.gov.uk*).

How to boost your company pension

To get a full company pension – limited to two-thirds of your final salary – normally it is necessary to work for 40 years for the same employer. This is because most company pensions build up at the rate of 1/60 of final salary for each year of service and the maximum is 40/60 or two-thirds (restricted in the case of some higher earners).

Today, very few employees follow this career pattern. Most change jobs a few times and spend at least some time out of employment to raise a family, in further education, as unemployed or self-employed and so on. This can have a serious impact on your pension, but it is possible to fill in the gaps in a tax-efficient way. The investments designed for this job are called 'additional voluntary contribution' schemes, where they are run by the employer, and 'free-standing' AVCs where they are set up on an individual basis by the employee. For the sake of brevity, in this chapter and elsewhere we use the accepted acronyms AVC and FSAVC.

Since April 2001 it has also been possible for members of occupational schemes who earn less than £30,000 to pay in to a personal pension. The £3,600 maximum contribution is in addition to the contribution limits for occupational schemes.

> Today, very few employees follow this career pattern. Most change jobs a few times and spend at least some time out of employment to raise a family, in further education, as unemployed or self-employed and so on.

What do AVCs and FSAVCs offer?

The first point to note about AVCs and FSAVCs is that they are approved pension arrangements and almost as tax-efficient as company schemes. That means:

- full tax relief on contributions
- tax-free growth of the fund
- in certain cases a tax-free cash lump sum at retirement, but only if you started payments before April 1988.

As with the main scheme, the pension itself is taxed as income. However, only employees can pay into an AVC scheme or an FSAVC plan. The employer usually does not contribute.

Generally you would take AVC benefits at retirement.

Stakeholder/personal pensions

Where you contribute to a personal pension you can take up to 25 per cent of the fund as tax-free cash and you can draw the benefits any time between the ages of 50 and 75. You can also continue contributions when you stop working for a further five years.

Your employer's AVC scheme

This is a company top-up scheme set up by the employer or trustees to run in conjunction with the main scheme. However, in most cases the investment and administration of the AVC scheme are sub-contracted to a third party. The majority of AVC schemes are run by the life offices and, in the case of deposit-style accounts, by the building societies. There are also a few unit trust and investment trust companies in the market.

The choice of provider is usually left to the trustees of the main pension scheme and research from actuarial consultants indicates that they don't always take this particular role very seriously. This is unfortunate because the difference in results between the best and worst company can knock about 20 per cent off the value of your fund.

The contract or agreement to make AVC payments is between the employee and the employer, so if you want to check any details you must go to the trustees or pensions manager. Before joining, therefore, you should ask them on what criteria the selection of the AVC provider was based and how often the scheme is monitored. If the trustees are doing a good job, they will have access to the latest surveys on AVC performance. If your AVC company is not in the top ten for performance and charges, you should ask why.

It is also important to check how flexible your contributions can be. Ideally you should be able to pay what you like, when you like, within Revenue limits of course. But some life offices are likely to lock you in to regular monthly contributions, and if you stop or reduce payments you might be penalized (for details of how these charges work, see Chapter 11). This is another important point to check before signing up.

How does it work?

Most AVCs operate on a 'money purchase' basis. This means that although the main scheme may provide a pension linked to salary, the AVC scheme is likely to invest the contributions to build up a fund which, at retirement, is used to buy an annuity from a life office. This annuity provides a guaranteed income for life, but the value of the annuity is dependent on the investment returns achieved by the AVC fund and has no link to the value of your final salary (see Chapter 19).

Some AVC schemes – mainly those in the public sector – offer 'added years'. This means that contributions buy extra 'years' in the main scheme where the pension is salary-linked (see Chapter 19, page 158). The advantage of added years is that the pension you buy has a known value and is likely to be inflation-linked automatically while you are in the scheme. This is because it forms part of the main pension scheme benefit which increases in line with earnings inflation through the link with the employee's final salary. Having said that, the opportunity to buy added years is becoming less common and even where it is available, the cost can be high.

FSAVCs are individual contracts between the employee and the plan provider. The employer and scheme trustee are not involved, and do not even need to know about the arrangement unless you are paying very high contributions. As with AVCs, the FSAVC market is dominated by the life assurance companies (there are almost 100 of these), although again a few unit trust and investment trust groups also offer this product.

Personal pension vs AVC vs FSAVC

If you earn less than £30,000 a year then consider paying into a stakeholder version of a personal pension. Your employer may offer one or you can pay in directly (see stakeholder pensions, page 182). As mentioned, personal pensions/stakeholders are more flexible than AVCs and you can take part of your fund as tax-free cash.

Although similar in many respects, there are some important differences between company AVCs and FSAVCs. FSAVCs are as flexible as company AVCs in terms of contributions, although in both cases, if the scheme is run by a life office it is important to find out exactly what charges you are paying and whether there are any penalties for stopping or reducing contributions.

At first glance, there seems little merit in looking outside the company scheme for a top-up arrangement, particularly since in many cases the employer helps to offset some or all of the AVC administration costs imposed by the life assurance company. Certainly if you are paying less than £50 a month, it is unlikely to be economic to take out an FSAVC.

> **If you are paying less than £50 a month, it is unlikely to be economic to take out an FSAVC – stick to your employer's AVC.**

The chief selling point of FSAVCs is their investment scope. While most larger company schemes offer an investment choice under their own AVC arrangements, there are many schemes which provide a single AVC option, often a deposit-style account run by a building society, or a 'with profits' fund run by a life office. For a full description of the different types of fund, see Chapter 21, page 188.

How much can you pay in?

If you are eligible to pay into a personal pension, the £3,600 annual limit is in addition to your company scheme/AVC contribution limit.

Despite the fact that AVCs and FSAVCs look very different from the main company scheme, it is misleading to regard them as a totally separate investment. In fact, the only time you can pay in to an AVC or FSAVC is when you are a member of a company scheme, while the amount you can pay in is dictated by the level of your contributions to the main scheme.

Under the Revenue rules, you can pay a total of 15 per cent of your earnings into the main scheme and AVC/FSAVC combined. Since most employees pay about 5 per cent, this leaves up to 10 per cent for the top-up scheme. If you are lucky enough to belong to a 'non-contributory' scheme, where the employer is the only one paying contributions, you can in theory invest the full 15 per cent of earnings into your AVC/FSAVC.

Some employees will be caught by the 'earnings cap', introduced by the 1989 Budget, which limits total pension contributions to 15 per cent of £95,400 (for the 2001–2002 tax year). The earnings cap affects employees who joined a new occupational scheme set up after March 14, 1989 and for new members who joined an existing scheme after June 1, 1989.

Finally on this point, if you accidentally exceed the benefit limits, the AVC/FSAVC provider can refund excess contributions, but a tax deduction must be paid to the Revenue.

How you take the proceeds

The rules here are unnecessarily complicated due to the introduction of various restrictions over the years. It all depends on when you started paying contributions.

Personal pensions

Here you can take the benefits at any time between the ages of 50 and 75. You can take up to 25 per cent of the fund as tax-free cash and must use the rest to buy an annuity. You may also take income withdrawals directly from the fund, but 'drawdown' is an expensive and complicated arrangement and is not suitable for small funds (under £100,000 in the case of pension top-up funds (see page 203)). An alternative is an investment-linked annuity (see page 202).

AVCs

- Where AVC contributions began before April 8, 1987, the whole fund can be taken in cash, provided the total cash taken from AVC and main scheme combined is within Revenue limits.

- From March 17, 1987, the Revenue restricted the level of salary on which the tax-free cash calculation was based. The ceiling was £100,000, so that the maximum cash taken from AVC and main scheme pension combined was £150,000 (one and a half times the £100,000 salary limit).

- Where contributions to the AVC scheme started on or after April 8, 1987, the whole of the fund must be taken in the form of pension, although its value is taken into consideration when the tax-free cash from the main scheme is calculated.

- Since FSAVCs were introduced only in 1987, there is no tax-free cash option.

So far the benefits all relate to pension. It is possible, however, to use part of your AVC allowance to buy additional life assurance. As with personal pension life assurance, effectively the premiums are tax-free.

Flexibility

Do check your FSAVC plan for flexibility and portability. As with a personal pension, you should be able to stop and start contributions, and increase or decrease payments without any financial penalty. If you change jobs you should be able to make the plan paid-up (i.e. terminate payments) or adapt it to your new needs.

If you are in doubt over your long-term employment plans, follow the golden rule of flexibility and pay for your advice by fees or pay single premium (one-off) contributions rather than commit yourself to a regular premium plan, which can give rise to hefty penalties if you are unable to keep up contributions for some reason.

Individual savings accounts as pension top-ups

In theory, you could use any savings plan as a pension top-up, but advisers reckon the most suitable and tax-efficient alternative to personal pensions and AVCs is an individual savings account. Isas are discussed in Chapter 12, so this section is restricted to their use as top-ups.

The tax efficiency of Isas is different but arguably comparable with AVCs, and as such they represent a sensible method of topping up a company pension and dealing with the 'earnings cap'. Indeed for some investors Isas will appear more attractive than the traditional top-up pensions.

In terms of tax-efficiency, with both AVCs and Isas the fund rolls up virtually free of income and capital gains tax, but in other respects the tax treatment differs. For example, AVCs qualify for full tax relief on contributions, but most of the benefits must be used to buy an annuity to provide a taxable income. With an Isa, there is no tax relief on contributions, but the fund can be withdrawn tax-free and does not have to be used to buy an annuity. Moreover, you have free access to the Isa fund whenever you like.

Higher earners in certain company schemes and those who have personal pensions are caught by the earnings cap. These investors can use Isas to build up a retirement fund to cover earnings in excess of the cap.

Summary

- Some company AVC schemes offer 'added years' but in most cases AVCs simply build up a fund which is used to buy an annuity to provide an income in retirement.

- Personal pensions, particularly the low-cost stakeholders, may be more attractive and flexible than AVCs for those earning less than £30,000.

- AVCs usually are better value than FSAVCs because the employer pays for some or all of the charges.

- Consider the investment options carefully. Younger employees should invest in a with profits or managed unit-linked or unit trust fund rather than a deposit-style account.

- If you want an FSAVC, seek independent financial advice to make sure you get the best value in terms of charges and performance.

- Check that the trustees monitor the company AVC scheme regularly to assess the performance. Ask to see details of comparisons with other companies.

- Flexibility is very important. Check that you can stop or reduce contributions whenever you want to without penalty.

- If you do not want a plan which locks away your investment until retirement, consider an Isa for medium- to long-term investment.

Glossary of terms

Additional voluntary contributions are tax-efficient schemes run by employers and are used to top up your main company pension.

Free-standing AVCs are individual plans used for the same purpose.

Individual savings accounts are not pensions but make ideal long-term retirement savings vehicles and are very flexible.

Personal pensions are also individual pension plans and provide an element of tax-free cash as well as an annuity.

Personal pensions and stakeholder schemes

In April 2001 the new stakeholder pension schemes became available. This scheme is a type of personal pension that is strictly regulated by the government to ensure it offers fair terms, low costs and penalty-free entry and exit.

With stakeholders came a new tax regime that applies to all personal pension plans. This is explained below, but the most important feature is that it breaks the link between earnings and pension contributions so that everyone under the age of 75 – including children and non-working adults – can have a plan, provided of course they have the money to fund it.

> **Stakeholders are intended to encourage people who have not had a private pension to save for retirement.**

Stakeholders are intended to encourage people who have not had a private pension to save for retirement. From October 2001, most employers who do not already offer a company scheme and who have five or more employees must make a stakeholder scheme available and be prepared to deduct contributions through the payroll. You may also join a stakeholder scheme directly. Your employer may contribute to your stakeholder personal pension but is not obliged to do so.

With their low charges – the maximum annual charge for stakeholder personal pensions is 1 per cent – and their ability to accept low contributions (anything from £20 per month), these new pension plans are ideal for lower earners. However, the rules will also appeal to wealthier people who want to set aside money in a pension for their children and, perhaps, for a non-working spouse.

Stakeholder pension schemes are registered with the Occupational Pensions Regulatory Authority (Opra, *www.stakeholder.opra.gov.uk*).

It is important to bear in mind that some personal pensions that do not qualify for stakeholder status offer equally good value. It is also vital to consider the long-term performance prospects. For higher earners who intend to pay substantial contributions, the charges arguably are less important than performance.

How much can you contribute?

The maximum contribution is £3,600 for 2001–2002 and anyone under the age of 75 can pay this into a personal pension, irrespective of whether they have any earned income.

This figure includes tax relief at the basic rate. For example, if you made a contribution of £2,808 this would be increased to £3,600 by way of a refund of tax from the Inland Revenue (assuming a basic rate of tax of 22 per cent). The tax relief is credited even if you do not pay tax, which is why this is so attractive for non-earners.

If you have earnings that entitle you to pay more than this you can do so provided you do not exceed the percentage of earnings shown on page 185, which starts at 17.5 per cent for those aged up to 35 and rises to 40 per cent for those over 61.

Tax efficient

Like company pension schemes, personal plans are a very tax-efficient way of saving for retirement:

- contributions qualify for full tax relief
- the pension fund grows virtually free of tax
- up to 25 per cent of the pension fund at retirement can be taken as tax-free cash (this does not apply to the plan used to contract out of Serps). The rest of the fund must be used to purchase an annuity.

FINANCIAL SNAPSHOT

Investment trust personal pensions do not qualify for stakeholder status but can offer very good value for money. You have to pay stamp duty on investment trusts which pushes up the cost in the first year but from year two the charges tend to be very low.

How to get the best value

With the help of a good independent financial adviser you should be able to narrow down your choice of pension companies by considering the following:

- the financial strength of the provider: it is important to be confident your pension company can survive – this very competitive market is in the throes of merger mania
- the performance track record, with the emphasis on consistency over the long term and stability of staff
- the level of charges deducted throughout the investment period (this is a maximum of 1 per cent per annum for stakeholders)
- the flexibility of the contract, for example, there should be no penalties for reducing and stopping contributions, transferring the fund and early retirement. This is guaranteed with stakeholder schemes.

Contracting out of SERPS

Personal pensions can also be used to contract out of the state earnings-related pension scheme on an individual basis, and in return receive a rebate of National Insurance contributions to invest in a plan of your choice. Employees who are not members of a contracted-out group scheme automatically are in Serps. (For more details on Serps, see Chapter 18.)

Your 'appropriate' personal pension (the rather daft technical name for plans used to contract out of Serps) can be bolted on to your main plan, or you could choose a different pension company. Spreading risk by investing with more than one company is a good idea in theory, but seek advice because the charges may outweigh the benefits if your contributions are small.

Employees who do not have access to an occupational scheme and those whose company scheme is not itself contracted out of Serps need to decide whether they will get better value from staying in Serps or opting out and investing the rebate of National Insurance contributions the Department of Social Security pays. (The self-employed do not pay into Serps, and so cannot take out an appropriate personal pension.)

Unfortunately Serps is being phased out, so the decision is complicated by uncertainty. All you can do is assume the government will pay the full value of the Serps pension you have earned when you retire (see page 153).

Comparing the value of what your Serps benefits would be worth with the value of what you might get if you invest the rebate is a job for actuaries, not mere mortals. From April 1997, the government is recalculating the rebates so that they reflect what Serps would be worth at any age. This means that age is no longer a reason for opting out or going back (in theory anyway). Assuming you have no political bias on the issue, probably the main factor to consider is your level of earnings. If you earn less than £15,000 a year (some insurance companies suggest a much lower pivotal salary) you probably should stay in Serps, because your rebate will be worth about £600 or less and you will find that most providers' charges will render this level of single premium uneconomic, unless you are making substantial top-up payments yourself. However, where you invest in a stakeholder scheme the charges will have less of an impact.

> Unfortunately the future of Serps is not assured and the chances are it will be phased out gradually. However, political uncertainty is an unreliable factor on which to base decisions.

The other point to remember is that the regulators have issued guidance to pension companies recommending that employees should opt out only if it is sensible to do so for a minimum of three years. This is for the same reason mentioned above – it simply isn't worth opting out for one year and leaving £600 with a life office for the next 20 before you retire.

For the actuarially minded, the rebate is calculated as a percentage of an employee's 'band earnings' – that is, earnings between the lower and upper threshold for NI contributions. For the 2001–2002 tax year the NI thresholds are £4,524 and £29,900 per annum, giving band earnings of £25,376. From April 1997, the fully age-related rebates start as low as 3.4 per cent of band earnings at age 16 and rising in stages to 9 per cent at age 46. So, if you are earning £29,900 or more the maximum rebate ranges from about £860 at age 16 to about £2,280 at age 46 or older.

The rebate is sent by the DSS direct to your personal pension provider after the end of the tax year to which it relates. It is always worth checking that your provider receives this promptly since a delay in investment will reduce the returns.

What can you buy with your fund?

The fund built up from the NI rebates is known as 'protected rights' – another daft name because the fund's value is not protected or guaranteed in any way: what you get depends on how well it is invested.

There are certain restrictions on what you can do with the fund at retirement. It cannot be used to provide tax-free cash, and the pension must be taken at the same age as the state pension, currently 65 for men and 60 for women (rising to 65 by the year 2020). The annuity purchased with the fund must provide for a spouse's pension worth 50 per cent of the personal pension planholder's and the annuity payments must increase by 3 per cent per annum. There are no restrictions on the annuity you purchase with your top-up plan.

Standard personal pensions

In addition to the rebate, you can and should contribute a significant proportion of your earnings into a personal pension since the rebate plan by itself will not provide an adequate pension. If you want to pay more than £3,600 a year you will base your maximum contributions on what the Inland Revenue calls 'net relevant earnings', which are roughly equivalent to annual earnings from any self-employed activities (after deducting losses and certain business charges on income) or from employment where either there is no company pension scheme or you have chosen not to join the company pension scheme.

The annual contribution limits are shown in Table 21.1 (but see 'High earners' below).

You can run more than one standard personal pension plan or stakeholder provided total contributions fall within these limits, but do consider the impact of start-up charges. However, you can have only one appropriate plan for each tax year.

Table 21.1 Annual contribution limits for top-up personal pensions

Age	% net relevant earnings*
Up to 35	17.5
36–45	20
46–50	25
51–55	30
56–60	35
61–74	40

* All personal pension contributions (but not the emerging pension itself) are subject to the earnings cap which limits the amount of salary that can be used for pension purposes to £95,400 for the 2001–2002 tax year.

Make sure that you are paying in a sensible amount each year – broadly between 6 and 16.5 per cent, depending on age. Your adviser should be able to help you assess the right contribution level. This will depend on how much pension you need and whether you have other sources of income. (See Table 19.1 on page 168 which shows how much you must pay in if you want to have a pension comparable to that available under a company final salary scheme.)

Don't forget – employers can contribute to an individual employee's plan, although there is no legal requirement for them to do so.

High earners

High earners with personal pensions are restricted by the 'earnings cap', introduced in the 1989 budget, which limits the amount of salary that can be taken into consideration for contributions.

For the 2001–2002 tax year, the cap is £95,400 which means that the maximum contribution for an employee aged under 35 is 17.5 per cent of the cap – £16,695. In practice, it is hard to see how this would act as a restriction for younger people who tend to be financially stretched by family commitments and mortgage repayments. Older employees, however, often pay higher contributions if they have made little provision earlier in life.

Making extra large contributions

There used to be something called 'carry forward' which allowed you to bring forward unused tax relief from up to six years earlier and make a higher contribution in the current year. This facility was withdrawn with effect from April 6, 2001.

What you can do, however, is use the 'carry back' facility. This allows you to ask the Inland Revenue to treat a contribution you are making now as if it had been paid in the previous tax year. This means that if you didn't make use of your full pension contribution entitlement in the previous year, you can catch up.

Until January 31, 2002, it is possible to use the carry forward and carry back provisions together to pay extra contributions. Ask your pension provider or adviser if you want to make a particularly large contribution.

Life assurance

It is also possible to use up to 5 per cent of the contribution limit to pay for life assurance, which effectively gives you tax relief on the premiums. Life assurance rates vary considerably, so shop around. If your pension provider's terms are expensive, it might be cheaper to buy it elsewhere.

Retirement annuities

Many people still have a retirement annuity plan – the predecessor to the personal pension. After July 1988 sales of these contracts stopped, but existing policyholders can continue to contribute to their plans.

The contribution and benefit rules for retirement annuities differ slightly from those for personal pensions. Retirement annuity contribution limits are lower in terms of percentages than for personal pensions, but the total salary on which these contributions are based is not subject to the earnings cap. The limits are shown in Table 21.2.

Table 21.2 Limits for retirement annuity contributions

Age	% net relevant earnings*
Up to 50	17.5
51–55	20
56–60	22.5
61–74	27.5

Depending on your age at retirement and the prevailing annuity rates, it may be possible to take more than 25 per cent of the retirement annuity fund as tax-free cash, since the calculation is not a straight percentage of the fund. The other main difference between the two arrangements is that you cannot contract out of Serps with one of these older contracts – you must use an appropriate personal pension.

Finally, it is possible to contribute to retirement annuities and personal pension plans at the same time, but you have to take care to keep within the Revenue's maximum contribution rules.

Who sells personal pensions?

It seems just about every financial institution is in this market, which makes the choice all the more difficult. However, the number of low-cost stakeholder providers was about 20 in April 2001 when they first became available. The market is dominated by the life offices, but an increasing number of unit trust and investment trust groups also offer plans and these are certainly worth considering. Most banks and building societies tend to

> Advisers tend to recommend that younger people should invest virtually 100 per cent in equities, because these offer the best long-term growth prospects.

sell the plans run by their own life office or have an arrangement with a separate life office to sell exclusively that company's plans. As in the Isa market, some of the big retail operations, such as M&S and Virgin, also sell pensions.

There are several investment options to consider – unit-linked, unit trust, investment trust, conventional 'with profits', unitized 'with profits' and guaranteed funds. Before you get bogged down with the different options, remember that the main consideration is the underlying asset mix. Advisers tend to recommend that younger people should invest virtually 100 per cent in equities, because these offer the best long-term growth prospects. As you get older and closer to retirement, you need to switch gradually into safer assets such as bonds and gilts and by the time you are within a few years of retirement you should probably be entirely in cash (deposits) and gilts.

Having said that, if you intend to transfer to an 'income-drawdown' plan at retirement, which allows you to keep your fund fully invested, you may be wise to maintain a high exposure to equities. This new retirement investment option is discussed on page 203.

Charges

Charges are discussed in Chapter 11. Do remember, if your adviser is paid a commission, to ask for your contributions to be classed as a series of single premiums or as 'recurring single premiums'. This means that each premium relates only to that particular payment so there are no heavy upfront deductions to cover commission costs for the full investment period. Over a 25-year plan, there would be little difference in total commission paid through regular and single premium plans. Where single premiums score is in flexibility. If you stop payments there are no early termination penalties.

Which fund?

Unit-linked plans

Unit-linked plans are sold by life offices. Under this arrangement, your contributions buy units in a fund and the value of these units fluctuates in line with the market value of the underlying assets. Funds range from low-risk deposit, index-linked and gilt, to medium-risk UK and international equity funds, to higher-risk emerging markets funds. Companies make much of their often huge fund range, but in practice most people go for the managed fund which invests in a range of the provider's other main funds and in this way offers a balanced spread of investments. An increasing number of companies – including stakeholder providers – offer investment links to top institutional managers. This is an excellent feature, but in non-stakeholder plans make sure the charges do not outweigh the potentially higher returns.

Stakeholder charges are limited to 1 per cent per annum. With other plans charges vary depending on the type of fund, but on average you can expect to pay an initial charge of about 5 per cent and an annual management charge of about 0.75 per cent to 1 per cent per annum (more – often double – if you use the plan to gain access to an external manager). On top of this, you may pay monthly policy charges. Sales commission, where applicable, will be included in the initial and annual charges.

Unit trust plans

Unit trust and open-ended investment company plans offer a similar investment choice to unit-linked plans, and again the value of your units will fluctuate in line with the performance of the underlying assets (see Chapter 11). The choice of unit trust personal pensions was limited to about half a dozen at the time of writing, but more plans may be launched over the next few years. Charges are similar to unit-linked funds, although the annual management charge may be higher. However, you can keep the bill down if you choose one of the index-tracking funds which generally offer access to a wide spread of equities at low cost, although you should look at ways to include overseas equities in your pension plan.

Investment trust plans

Over the past few years, a handful of investment trust personal pensions have been launched (see Chapter 11). An investment trust is not a trust as such but is a British company, listed on the UK Stock Exchange, which invests in the shares of other companies in the UK and overseas. It has a fixed number of shares, and most prices are published daily in the *Financial Times*.

The investment trust's share price is affected by the value of the company's underlying assets, as is the case with unit-linked and unit trust funds. However, it is also affected by the supply and demand for shares.

This means that the share price does not necessarily reflect the actual value of the underlying assets. If the share price is lower than the value of the underlying assets, the difference is known as the discount. If it is higher, the difference is known as the premium. Buying at a discount is a good thing, buying at a premium is generally considered to be a bad thing. Investment trusts can also borrow money to invest, an activity known as gearing.

As a broad rule of thumb, investment trusts offer additional opportunities for active investors but they are also potentially more volatile. Charges tend to be lower than for unit trusts (with the exception of index trackers), particularly on some of the larger older investment trusts.

'With profits' plans

Until recently, these worthy but ridiculously complicated funds formed the backbone of the individual pensions market because they provided a reasonable degree of security together with good potential for long-term capital growth.

The mystical path to understanding the with profits concept is littered with jargon. The with profits fund (which in fact is the fund of the life office itself) invests mainly in UK and international equities, gilts and fixed-interest securities and property. Under the original with profits contract (referred to by life offices as the 'traditional' or 'conventional' contract) the investor is guaranteed a substantial sum at the end of the investment period (known as the 'maturity' date) to which annual or 'reversionary' bonuses are added. The important point is that, rather like interest on a building society account, these bonuses are guaranteed and once allocated cannot be taken away.

The annual bonuses are 'smoothed' in order to provide a relatively consistent return. To do this, the life office holds back some of the profits in good years to boost returns in lean years. In this way, the plans tend to avoid the volatility associated with unit-linked and unit trust plans. On top of this there is a final or 'terminal' bonus which is discretionary, and tends to reflect actual performance over the past 12 months.

There are no explicit charges on a with profits plan apart from a monthly policy fee. This does not mean that you don't pay charges, it simply means that you can't work out how they are calculated. Generally the charges are deducted from the fund itself before the bonuses are declared – again rather like a building society account where charges are deducted before the interest rate is declared. Fortunately, now that companies must disclose in full the impact of their charges on your investment, it is possible to compare with profits fund charges with other types of personal pensions.

Unitized 'with profits' plans

Unitized with profits plans are supposed to occupy the middle ground between the conventional with profits structure and unit-linked funds. One advantage of this is that investors with unit-linked plans can more easily switch into the lower-risk unitized with profits fund – a common strategy in the run-up to retirement when you want to consolidate gains and reduce risk.

> Unitized with profits plans are supposed to occupy the middle ground between the conventional 'with profits' structure and unit-linked funds.

Unfortunately unitized plans are, if anything, even more complicated than their conventional predecessors. Under unitized contracts, there is no guaranteed sum assured and so the provider does not have to set aside such large reserves to meet its obligations. Furthermore, the bonuses are declared in a very different format from the traditional contract. Most providers increase the value of the unit price, but a minority maintain a fixed unit price, and add bonuses through the allocation of extra units. Within these two systems, there is a host of variations on the way profit is distributed.

Quite a few providers do not offer a guaranteed minimum bonus at all. As with the traditional contract, unitized funds also apply a final bonus.

Unitization also heralded the arrival of the controversial 'market value adjuster' (MVA). These adjusters are used as a safety net for life offices in the event of a mass exodus of clients following a drop in the markets – or public confidence, as happened with Equitable Life. Effectively, the MVA allows a company to reduce the value of units whenever it likes and by however much it wants. In this respect, the guaranteed nature of the annual bonuses is not rock solid after all.

It is worth noting that the stakeholder with profits funds are 'ring fenced' and do not participate in the profits of the life office as a whole.

Guaranteed equity funds

If you want exposure to equities but can't handle the white-knuckle ride of the stock markets, you might consider one of the relatively new 'guaranteed' funds which limit your exposure to falls in the stock market and provide a percentage of the gains.

Guaranteed equity funds are strange beasts, and in fact rarely invest in equities but instead hold mainly cash and gilts. The fund manager buys derivatives to guarantee a certain rise in the index and to limit the percentage of any fall in prices. Of course the guarantee does not come free. In effect, what you lose is the equivalent of the stock market dividend yield. When you consider the fact that over time the yield on the FTSE 100 index accounts for a substantial chunk of the total return, its absence seems a high price to pay.

However, experts argue that you could be compensated for the loss of yield by the fact that the fund limits your exposure to any falls in the index, so you gain from potentially greater capital growth than unprotected investors. This is particularly relevant in volatile market conditions.

Charges are higher than for most of the other funds mentioned here – largely because of the cost of the derivatives which provide the guarantee.

Anything to do with derivatives is bound to be complicated, and the jury is still out on whether these funds really do what they are supposed to do. The old investment adage 'if you don't understand it, don't invest in it' probably applies here, although there may be a strong argument in favour of using these funds for income drawdown plans, where you keep your pension fund fully invested in retirement (see page 203).

Transfers to personal pensions

Personal pension plans can be used to accept a transfer value from a company pension. This is a complex area and the subject of considerable controversy since the mass mis-selling of plans for this purpose in the late 1980s.

The mis-selling scandal

In December 1993, the Securities and Investments Board (SIB), the forerunner of the Financial Services Authority (FSA), revealed that most personal pension sales since 1988 were based on poor advice and that employees would have been better off with their company pension scheme benefits, many of which offer valuable guarantees.

Between one-quarter and one-half of the employees who transferred to personal plans came from local government and the public sector, which run some of the best pension schemes in the country. Estimates of the total bill for compensation run as high as £11bn, with average individual settlements of £8,000 to £10,000.

The motivation behind the mis-selling spree was simple greed. Insurance companies raked off huge profits to cover their administration and investment management costs. They also paid substantial commissions to sales representatives and independent advisers. All of which came out of the victims' pension funds.

In November 1996, the SIB decided to ditch the unworkable system it had introduced in 1993 to identify and compensate victims. The new campaign, which was started in Spring 1997, required almost all of the 570,000 investors identified to complete a detailed questionnaire about their company and personal pensions – information those selling the personal plans have largely failed to obtain.

How will the compensation be paid?

The regulators said that the aim of the review was 'to put investors back in the position in which they would have been if they had not taken out a personal pension'. The best outcome by far is to be fully re-instated in your pension scheme for the opt-out period. In this case the pension company will pay a lump sum, which will include the value of your personal pension, to your former pension scheme. Mind you, the FSA has no powers to force company schemes to accept re-instatement and where this is not possible – for example in the case of transfers of former benefits where you are no longer employed by that company – you are likely to be offered a guaranteed annuity which will replace lost benefits at retirement.

A third alternative is a top-up to your personal pension which, given the lack of guarantees, is not really satisfactory. Moreover, if you were sold a plan that combines high charges with poor performance, putting in more money only adds insult to injury. In this case you may wish to contest the offer or at least insist the money is paid into a plan with a more reputable company. Always seek expert advice.

Personal pension mortgages

It is possible to arrange to pay off your interest-only mortgage through a personal pension plan (see Chapter 16), making use of the tax-free cash on retirement to repay the outstanding capital. This may be worth considering if you do not already pay maximum contributions, because you effectively get tax relief on your mortgage repayment investment vehicle.

However, be careful not to undermine your pension at retirement, and make sure you are protected for periods of unemployment when you cannot continue pension payments. Finally, flexibility is essential. You need to be able to stop your

> Flexibility is essential. You need to be able to stop your personal pension without penalty if you change jobs and want to join your new employer's company scheme.

personal pension without penalty if you change jobs and want to join your new employer's company scheme.

Self-invested personal pensions (SIPPs)

Self-invested personal pensions follow the same basic rules as standard personal pensions, but in addition allow you to exercise much greater control over your investments. Like self-select Isas, the appeal of the SIPP lies in the product's ability to 'unbundle' the two key features of modern pension plans, namely the administration and the investment. What generally happens is that the administration is carried out by a specialist life office, and you either tackle the investment yourself or appoint an investment manager (a stockbroker, for example) to construct and run the portfolio for you. If you are unhappy with the performance you can change the manager without having to upset the underlying administration arrangements.

SIPPs can also be used by partnerships which are excluded from the company-sponsored small self-administered schemes but they can use a SIPP with virtually the same effect and, if they pool their contributions and funds, they can achieve beneficial economies of scale.

Investment choice

The choice of investments is wide and includes the following:

- stocks and shares (e.g. equities, gilts, debentures) quoted on the UK Stock Exchange and including securities on the Alternative Investment Market;
- stocks and shares traded on a recognized overseas exchange
- unit trusts and investment trusts
- insurance-company-managed funds and unit-linked funds
- deposit accounts
- commercial property.

A SIPP fund cannot purchase a firm's existing business premises from the partnership, but it can buy new offices into which the partnership can move, provided the property is leased back on a commercial basis. You can use your SIPP fund to borrow on the strength of its assets to help with property purchase. However, the SIPP cannot lend part of the pension fund back to you, the investor.

You can also invest in a 'hybrid' SIPP. Under a hybrid, it is necessary to pay a minimum contribution each year to the life office, which also provides the administration, while any contributions above this minimum can be invested however you wish under the full SIPP rules. Hybrids might prove attractive and cost-effective where lower contributions are paid, but once total annual contributions exceed, say, £10,000, then a pure SIPP is likely to provide the best value for money as well as offering maximum investment control.

Group personal pensions

Group personal pensions are becoming very popular among employers. Also, some affinity groups such as the trade unions and professional bodies offer 'industry-wide' GPPs. The providers are the same as for individual schemes – mainly the life offices, but also a few unit trust and investment trust groups. More recently, some of the heavyweight institutional fund managers have moved into this market – a welcome development, particularly where they bring with them a first-rate performance track record.

If your employer offers a group personal pension, see the section on group money purchase schemes which starts on page 166. This will help you decide whether the terms are flexible and offer good value for money. In particular, you should check the amount your employer is prepared to pay on your behalf, and whether there are any penalties if you reduce or stop your contributions when you change jobs.

At their most basic, group personal pensions are no more than a collection of individual plans. However, the more sophisticated schemes, usually negotiated by a consultant, make full use of the potential for economies of scale to reduce administration and investment charges. More generous plans feature employer contributions, death benefits and disability benefits. Whether your group plan is generous or not will depend on how much your employer is prepared to pay.

Ideally, your employer will arrange the group personal pension on a 'nil commission' basis. This means that the commission costs are stripped out and your employer's adviser is paid a fee. The main advantage of this system is a clear, flexible charging structure – you can see exactly what you are paying, and if you change the amount of contribution or stop paying altogether there is no penalty. With any luck, your employer may cover the charges and not pass them on to scheme members.

Summary

- Don't buy a standard personal pension if you have access to a good company pension scheme. Company pensions generally represent better value for money, and usually provide good death and disability benefits as well.

- If there is no company scheme, invest in a stakeholder or standard personal pension and try to get your employer to contribute as well.

- It may be worthwhile opting out of Serps with an 'appropriate' personal pension if you earn more than £15,000 a year.

- If you want a standard personal pension, independent financial advice is essential (see Chapter 1). Check the performance, charges and flexibility of the plan as well as the company's financial strength.

Glossary of terms

Appropriate personal pensions are used to accept the rebate of National Insurance contributions if you contract out of Serps.

Group personal pensions are a type of company scheme but in fact represent a series of individual plans.

Guaranteed funds use derivatives to limit your exposure to stock market volatility.

Income drawdown plans allow you to keep your personal pension fund fully invested in retirement up to age 75, while drawing a regular income.

Investment trust plans offer greater potential for the active investor but are potentially more volatile than unit-linked and unit trust plans.

Market value adjuster (MVA): These adjusters are used as a safety net for life offices in the event of a mass exodus of clients. Effectively the MVA allows a company to reduce the value of units whenever it likes and by however much it wants.

Net relevant earnings are broadly equivalent to annual earnings from any self-employed activities (after deducting losses and certain business charges on income).

Retirement annuity plans: The predecessor to the personal pension. After July 1988 sales of these contracts stopped but existing policyholders can continue to contribute.

Self-invested personal pensions allow you to separate the administration and investment management so you can change the manager without the expense of switching the whole plan.

Stakeholder schemes are personal pensions that must guarantee low costs, easy access and penalty-free entry and exit terms.

Unit-linked personal plans are sold by life offices. Your contributions buy units in a fund and the value of these units fluctuates in line with the market value of the underlying assets.

Unit trust personal plans are similar to unit-linked plans. Charges are clearer but tend to be slightly higher.

'With profits' plans invest in a mix of all asset classes and each year award a bonus or interest rate which, once added to your account, cannot be taken away. There are other bonuses, for example a discretionary final bonus at retirement. **Unitized** with profits invest in the with profits fund but on a unitized basis, so your contributions buy units.

Further information

The stakeholder register is at *www.stakeholder.opra.gov.uk* or you can phone 01273 627600.

How to buy your retirement income

An annuity provides a guaranteed income for life in return for a lump sum investment. If you have a money purchase (defined contribution) pension arrangement, where the level of your pension is not linked to your salary, at retirement you can usually take a hefty chunk as tax-free cash, but the rest must be used to buy an annuity to provide your retirement income.

> The annuity 'rate' – or the level of regular income you secure in return for your lump sum – will depend on several important factors, including your life expectancy and interest rates.

Annuities are sold by insurance companies. The annuity 'rate' – or the level of regular income you secure in return for your lump sum – will depend on several important factors including your life expectancy and interest rates. If you are in ill health, you may be able to get a better rate if the insurance company thinks your life expectancy is less than the average for your age.

Most annuities offer a fixed income, but a handful offer an investment link to a 'with profits' or unit-linked fund, so here the level of income will also be determined by how well your fund performs.

Independent advice essential

You are under no obligation to buy your annuity from the company with which you have your pension arrangement. The 'open market option' allows you to take the proceeds of your pension fund away from the plan provider and to buy your annuity elsewhere. The top names in personal pensions are quite different from the top names in annuities, so it pays to shop around. However, take into consideration any penalties or loyalty bonuses that affect your pension fund if you move it away from your original company.

Your choices at retirement

There are four broad options:

■ You can buy a conventional annuity from an insurance company. This provides a guaranteed income for life which can be fixed or can rise annually. The conventional annuity effectively locks you into current gilt yields.

■ If you have other sources of income, you can leave your pension fund in the pension plan until you are 75 at the latest. Your fund will continue to grow virtually tax-free but you will not be able to take your tax-free cash or draw an income.

■ You can buy an investment-linked annuity and hope to improve the level of your annuity income through good investment returns.

■ You can transfer to a drawdown plan, which offers full exposure to the stock markets as well as inheritance tax planning opportunities.

If you are moving into semi-retirement or you have a source of income – for example from investments or a family business – you may decide to leave your pension fund where it is for the time being. The most flexible home for a substantial fund is a self-invested personal pension, which allows you to invest directly in equities and bonds as well as in a wide choice of funds. You can stay in a SIPP or standard personal pension until the age of 75 when you have to convert the fund to an annuity. If you die while the fund is in the personal plan, the fund forms part of your estate and can be passed on to your dependants, so this is attractive from the inheritance tax perspective.

Assuming that you need to draw an income, you will have to 'vest' part or all of your pension plan. This means you can take the tax-free cash – usually about 25 per cent of the fund – and use the remainder to generate an income through an annuity or drawdown arrangement. It is important to remember you do not have to put all your eggs in one basket. It is possible to combine one or more of these options. For example, you may decide to use half your fund to lock in to the safety of a conventional annuity and with the other half buy an investment-linked annuity.

F I N A N C I A L   S N A P S H O T

Women tend to live longer than men, so usually receive a lower income in return for the same level of investment.

To find out more about your options, consult an independent adviser with pensions, tax and investment expertise.

Annuity options

The DSS applies certain rules to the type of annuity you must buy with the fund you build up from your rebates of National Insurance contributions (see page 185). But with the rest of the fund, there are no specific rules. There are, however, several useful features which are sold as optional extras to the basic annuity. Some of these may be essential, depending on your circumstances but they do reduce the annuity rate, so consider your priorities carefully.

- **Guaranteed annuities** guarantee to make payments for five years, and if you die during this period your beneficiaries will receive the outstanding amount.
- **Joint life basis** means that a full or reduced pension will be paid to your spouse if you die.
- **Escalating annuities** rise fully in line with retail price inflation or at a fixed rate each year, typically 3 per cent or 5 per cent. Given that you are likely to be retired for 20 years or more, some form of inflation-proofing is essential, but the cost is rather prohibitive. A 5 per cent annual increase, for example, would reduce the initial annuity rate by about one-third. If this sounds pricey, bear in mind that the purchasing power of £100 will be worth just £64 after 15 years of inflation at 3 per cent, and £48 if the inflation rate is 5 per cent. Several companies offer annuities linked to retail prices for about the same price as the 5 per cent fixed rate of inflation-proofing.

Guaranteed but inflexible

Annuities have serious drawbacks which 'phased retirement' and 'income drawdown' plans aim to overcome. With a conventional annuity, once you hand over your money, you cannot change your mind about the choice of insurance company or the special features selected. In most cases your money is gone for good, even if you die shortly afterwards. As mentioned above, you can protect your fund – usually for five years – but this costs extra.

If you are ready to buy and are prepared to shop around through a specialist annuity adviser, you are already well on your way towards getting the best deal. The difference between the best and worst annuity rates at any given time can be as much as 20 per cent.

Investing in real assets

Falling gilt yields and increasing longevity have forced down annuity rates substantially in recent years. According to specialist adviser The Annuity Bureau, in 1990 a 65-year-old man could have secured an annuity income of £11,000 per annum with a fund of £100,000. This would have included annual increases of 3 per cent and a spouse's pension worth half of his own on his death. By 1995 that annuity rate had dropped to about £8,000. If you had made the same purchase in 2000 you would have secured an annual income of just £6,000.

This perceived deterioration in annuity rates has encouraged those coming up to retirement to look for ways to avoid locking in to gilt yields and to maintain a link with real assets in the hope of improving their income, albeit at varying degrees of risk.

Investment-linked annuities

Most annuities offer a fixed or rising income, but an increasing number of companies offer annuities that invest your capital in a range of collective funds and link your income to the returns achieved. This type of product is still an annuity, so the fund reverts to the insurance company when you die apart from any arrangements you have made for your spouse. However, the income is boosted by the effect of 'annuitizing' – that is, taking advantage of the cross-subsidy from pooling mortality risk with other annuitants.

You may have some flexibility in setting the level of income at the outset, but if returns do not match your expectations your future income will fall. The way the income is calculated is complicated and varies from product to product and you should ask your adviser to explain this carefully.

As with any approved pension arrangement your fund continues to grow virtually tax-free. Most companies that sell investment-linked annuity products offer only their own fund range, from which you can select the geographical areas and sectors to suit your risk tolerance. The more progressive companies offer access to a range of external asset managers as well. These include Canada Life, Merchant Investors, Prudential and Scottish Widows.

Several other companies offer with profits annuities. Here your capital is invested in the company's own with profits fund, which offers a mixed asset allocation (usually about two-thirds in equities, the rest in bonds, gilts, cash and property) and may provide limited guarantees to maintain a basic income level. Returns are smoothed to avoid excessive volatility.

The with profits fund is considered a lower risk alternative to unit-linked funds where the value of your units rises and falls directly in line with the underlying assets. While the with profits structure has been criticized in recent years for lack of transparency and the significant asset allocation to gilts and bonds, advisers suggest it is worth considering in retirement. The real downside of unit-linked funds is volatility. In retirement, with profits is an appropriate option for some investors because it reduces risk. Other companies that offer with profits annuities include Legal & General, Norwich Union, Standard Life and Sun Life.

Some investment-linked annuity providers allow you to convert to a conventional annuity at any time up to the age of 85, although you cannot move to a different provider at this point.

Phased retirement

Until 1996, the main alternative to a conventional annuity was phased retirement where you generate your required annual income by withdrawing only part of your pension fund, leaving the remaining fund invested. The chunk withdrawn is used to provide an element of tax-free cash and the rest is used to buy an annuity. The pattern is repeated each year.

Phased retirement is not suitable for investors who want to use their tax-free cash for a capital project, because in the plan this is used instead to make up part of the income. However, if you don't need the lump sum, phased retirement may be suitable. It also offers full tax-free cash to your beneficiaries on death (avoiding inheritance tax), and it can be easier to change your investment manager than under the newer income drawdown plans, where this is possible only through the self-invested version.

> Phased retirement is not suitable for investors who want to use their tax-free cash for a capital project, because in the plan this is used instead to make up part of the income.

Income drawdown plans

Income drawdown plans can offer a welcome degree of flexibility compared with conventional annuities. Moreover, with income drawdown, you take control of both the timing and the amount of your income payments and at the same time keep your fund fully invested in a tax-free environment.

Of course, there is a catch. Income drawdown plans are marketed as the ultimate in flexible retirement planning, and as any seasoned financial adviser will tell you, 'flexible' in investment terms usually is synonymous with 'complicated' and 'risky'.

Taking a risk while you are young may be acceptable, but it poses serious problems in retirement when you have no earnings to fall back on if your savings are decimated by poor investment returns, high sales commissions and substantial running costs. So, before you take the plunge, make sure you understand the downside of income drawdown as well as the potential benefits.

Under income drawdown plans, you can still take your tax-free cash and then draw your taxable income direct from your fund. The income level is flexible, although it must fall between a minimum and maximum set by the Inland Revenue, based broadly on the annuity rate you would otherwise have secured with your fund at retirement. Within the pension fund, your investments continue to grow free of income and capital gains tax. If you die, your fund goes to your dependants, not the insurance company, so there are important tax and financial planning benefits as well. By age 75 at the latest, you must convert your fund to an annuity.

So far the odds in favour of income drawdown look good. However, the main risk with these plans is that, whereas with conventional annuities your pension income is guaranteed, with income withdrawal it is not.

You might think that you could make your position more secure by investing in something fairly safe – gilts and deposits, for example. However, in most cases this would defeat the object of the exercise, which is to generate a return that will match or improve the income you would have received from an annuity. Annuity rates are based on medium- and long-dated gilts, which at the time of writing were yielding about 8.5 per cent per annum. So there is your absolute minimum target return, on top of which you must allow for investment and administration costs, which will set you back at least 1.5 per cent a year.

Mortality drag

There is also a rather important but obscure factor called 'mortality drag'. Basically, annuities work like an insurance pool – those who live get a cross-subsidy from those who die. Under income withdrawal, you get your money back if you die, but you lose this cross-subsidy, which experts reckon is worth about 1.5–2 per cent a year. In total, therefore, you are looking for returns of about 12 per cent minimum, and the only sensible way to achieve this is to invest in an equity fund.

And therein lies the rub. If markets fall, your fund will plummet and take your retirement income with it. Clearly, if the fund was your only source of pension, you could end up in deep trouble. The only way out would be to invest in even higher-risk funds, and then the white-knuckle ride starts to get really scary.

Advisers recommend that you should not consider these plans unless you have substantial funds. This means a minimum of £100,000 in your pension pot, and plenty of other assets to support you in retirement if your pension fund falls in value. If you don't have other assets, you probably shouldn't consider income drawdown, unless your pension fund is worth at least £200,000 to £250,000. Some advisers suggest £500,000.

> If the fund was your only source of pension, you could end up in deep trouble. The only way out would be to invest in even higher-risk funds, and then the white-knuckle ride starts to get really scary.

You also need good-quality advice. This is a very technical area, so your adviser must have expert back-up to cover all the pensions, investment and taxation aspects.

Phased drawdown

These arrangements combine phased retirement with income drawdown and so use the tax-free cash to generate part of the income. If you don't need your cash lump sum, this is considered the most flexible arrangement, but seek expert advice.

How to choose

There are several ways of setting up an income drawdown plan. First, you can buy an insurance company package that combines administration and investment management. A second option, widely favoured by advisers, is to separate these two features and run the fund yourself or appoint an investment manager to do the job for you (rather like a self-invested personal pension – see page 194). A third option is to go for a 'guaranteed' fund which limits the downside of stock market risk – but at a price (see below).

Buying from an insurance company

The first route – buying an insurance company package – is attractive from the point of view of simplicity. However, once you take your tax-free cash and start to withdraw an income, you cannot transfer your fund to another provider. If your plan restricts you to the internal funds of just one insurer, you are stuck with that company – and its investment performance – until you buy your annuity. Hardly prudent, given the fact that you could be investing for 15 to 20 years. Packaged products are sold by about 20 life offices, although several also offer a choice of external fund management links.

Complete flexibility

Where you want complete flexibility over the investment management, and your fund size justifies the cost, you should consider the 'self-invested' route which separates the administration and investment management. This means you can run the fund yourself or appoint an investment manager to do the job for you. If you are unhappy with the performance, you can change your manager while leaving the administration intact. Under this type of plan, you can invest in a very wide range of funds and asset classes, including collective funds (investment trusts, unit trusts and insurance company funds), direct equities, bonds and commercial property.

Normally the administration would be carried out by an insurance company, although some financial institutions run their own plans and may also offer a discretionary investment management service, although this is not obligatory.

Guaranteed funds

Another option you might consider is a 'guaranteed' fund which limits your exposure to falls in the stock market and provides a percentage of the gains. This type of fund may be attractive to retired investors who need exposure to equity markets but who can't afford to take the risks. (For further details on guaranteed funds, see page 191).

Plan your exit carefully

Finally, remember that the hallmark of good investment planning is knowing in advance when to get out. Under income withdrawal, by age 75 at the latest you must buy your annuity. To identify the best time to make your purchase, you need to keep an eye on equity prices, which affect your fund size, and on gilt prices, which determine the level of income your annuity will provide. Generally, when equity prices go up, gilt prices also rise. This means gilt yields fall taking annuity rates with them.

So, what you want is a rise in equity prices and a fall in gilt prices – but it rarely works out that way. Clearly, trying to spot the right conjunction of equity and gilt movements is rather like astrology and best left to the experts.

Conclusion and warning

Conventional annuities offer a rock-solid guarantee and represent the best option for those who will depend solely or mainly on this income. Shopping around for the best conventional annuity rate is essential. Think very carefully before you commit yourself to an income drawdown plan – or similar arrangement – which exposes your retirement fund to stock market risks.

Purchased life annuities

Most people come across annuities when they retire and must buy a compulsory annuity with the proceeds of their pension fund. There is, however, a second type, known as a 'purchased life' or 'voluntary' annuity, which anyone can buy with their spare capital.

INCOME DRAWDOWN PLAN RULES

If you have a personal pension or similar plan, at retirement you can take part of the fund (typically one-quarter) as tax-free cash and use the rest to buy an annuity. If you choose to defer the annuity purchase using a new income drawdown plan, the following rules apply:

■ You can buy the plan from age 50, but must convert the fund to an annuity by age 75.

■ You cannot make further pension contributions to the plan once it is in operation.

■ During the deferment period, investment income and capital gains continue to roll up tax-free.

■ The income you draw must fall between a minimum and maximum set by the Inland Revenue and be based on the annuity rate you would have purchased had you converted your fund at retirement.

■ Your plan must be reviewed every three years to ensure the income level you are drawing is still appropriate. If the fund has fallen too much, you must convert to an annuity immediately.

■ If you die before age 75, there are three options:
  i) Your spouse can use the fund to buy an annuity.
  ii) Your spouse can continue to draw an income but must convert the fund to an annuity by the time you would have reached 75.
  iii) The fund can be taken as cash (less a 35 per cent tax charge).

Summary

- Shop around – the best annuity rates on the market at any given time can be 25 per cent more than the worst.
- Check whether your pension company applies any penalties if you buy elsewhere or adds any loyalty bonuses if you stay put. Take these into consideration when shopping around.
- Seek expert advice. Your adviser should specialize in annuities, and have the necessary software to check all the products available.
- Consider carefully which features you need, for example a spouse's pension and inflation-proofing.
- Think carefully before opting for an investment-linked annuity since your income is not guaranteed and will fluctuate in line with investment returns.
- Consider income drawdown, but only if you have a substantial fund and other sources of income. You must also feel comfortable with the equity market risks involved.

Glossary of terms

Annuities provide an income for life in return for a lump sum investment.

Compulsory purchase annuities: If you have a personal pension or similar plan, you must use most of the proceeds to buy this type of annuity.

Income drawdown allows you to keep your pension fund fully invested in retirement up to the age of 75 and to draw an income from your fund.

Investment-linked annuities offer the opportunity to increase your income through stock market growth but are much more risky than conventional annuities.

Phased retirement operates like income drawdown, but here you use your tax-free cash to generate part of your income.

Purchased life annuities can be bought voluntarily with spare capital.

Working and retiring abroad

The whole area of expatriate pensions is in the throes of change and unless you are confident that your company provides the best possible arrangement in terms of value and security, it is wise to seek expert advice before signing up for that overseas assignment.

This chapter looks at the pension problems facing all UK expatriates, in particular arrangements within the European Union, then focuses on retiring abroad and taking your pensions with you.

One of the main problems for expatriates seconded within the European Union (and virtually anywhere else, for that matter) is the absence of a workable cross-border pensions regime. The tax structure of pension schemes is complicated enough on a national level, but when more than one regime is involved, the system breaks down and the tax officials engage in a free-for-all.

> One of the main problems for expatriates seconded within the European Union (and virtually anywhere else, for that matter) is the absence of a workable cross-border pensions regime.

Most European pension systems work on the basis of tax deferment. This means that there is tax relief on contributions and the build-up of the pension fund, but all or most of the pension itself is taxed in full as income. Quite understandably, if a country grants tax relief on contributions, it will be keen to claim the tax on the pension itself. If it does not, a fiscal imbalance arises.

Clearly it is essential to know your rights, to understand the impact of a foreign assignment on your pension, and to be sufficiently well-informed to negotiate the best possible deal for yourself and your family.

The following details cover the main aspects to consider when negotiating your expatriate pensions package. However, bear in mind that these points offer general guidance only. Your contract should relate specifically to the actual assignment and must be tailored to cater for any particular problem areas.

Foreign state pensions

The UK pays a rather miserly pension, but elsewhere in Europe the benefits are much higher. In some countries – Spain and Greece, for example – the pension is worth more than 90 per cent of national average earnings, so it is important to keep track of any rights you build up to foreign state pensions since these may provide a valuable source of income in retirement.

Assessing the value of overseas state pensions is not easy. Different countries apply different qualifying periods which set out the minimum number of years you must pay into the local national insurance system before a pension can be claimed. In the UK it is normally necessary to work and pay full National Insurance contributions for at least ten years before you qualify for a proportion of the basic state pension, although benefits under Serps build up from day one. In Belgium, an employee qualifies for a proportion of the state pension after just one year, whereas in Luxembourg, as in the UK, the minimum qualifying period is 10 years, and in Portugal and Spain the qualifying minimum is set even higher, at 15 years.

Fortunately, the EU has an excellent system in place which is designed to ensure that expatriate employees do not lose out on their state pension rights as a result of single or multiple assignments within the member states.

As a general rule, when you work abroad for more than one year (technically, from day one) you must pay National Insurance or social security contributions in the country of assignment. There are a few exceptions to this, particularly where the assignment is expected to last for less than a year, or where the work covers several countries, in which case it may be possible to stay in the UK scheme.

Assuming, however, that your assignments are for a longer period, the Multilateral Agreement on Social Security allows you to combine the total number of years worked in the EU in order to meet minimum qualifying periods in each country.

To complicate matters further, state pension ages vary from country to country and payment of the pension is usually dealt with by each country's social security department and paid in local currency. Each element of the

FINANCIAL SNAPSHOT

The European Union has tried hard to create a pan-EU pensions structure for so-called 'mobile' or expatriate workers, but so far has only really helped employees who are seconded abroad by an employer and stay with that company.

pension is subject to the annual increases that apply in the country of source.

For the expatriate whose career spans several countries, it can be something of an administrative nightmare keeping track of all these foreign state pensions, particularly where governments are in the process of changing the benefit structure to reduce costs. To avoid problems later, keep track of your social security number and the period you worked. Supply these details to the relevant authorities at retirement. Outside the Euro zone payments in different currencies will lead to fluctuations in terms of the pensions' purchasing power.

> For the expatriate whose career spans several countries, it can be something of an administrative nightmare keeping track of all these foreign state pensions, particularly where governments are in the process of changing the benefit structure to reduce costs.

State pensions outside the EU

While the details above refer specifically to the EU, it is worth noting that the UK has social security agreements with many countries around the world, so claiming your state pension should not present any serious problems. For details on payment of a UK pension overseas contact the DSS.

Company pensions

For your main company pension, there are several options to consider, including remaining in the UK scheme, joining the local scheme in the country of assignment, and setting up an offshore scheme or plan.

Retention in UK scheme

The important point to note about private pension schemes in the UK – whether set up by an employer or by an individual – is that under normal circumstances you can contribute only if you have UK earnings. These 'relevant earnings' are defined very clearly by the Inland Revenue, and as a rule do not include earnings paid by an employer while you are working abroad.

Stakeholder pension contributions are not linked to earnings but at the time of writing it was too early to assess whether temporary expats would be able to use a UK stakeholder while working abroad.

Fortunately, the UK tax authorities have one of the most flexible attitudes to employees who work abroad, and generally it is possible to remain in the

UK company scheme for at least five years, provided your employer meets certain qualifying rules. The advantages of this arrangement are obvious, particularly if you plan to retire in the UK. All your benefits come from one source in one currency and you do not have to track down pension benefits from foreign employers when you come to retire in 20 years' time.

Foreign company schemes

If you are going abroad to work for a foreign employer, you should also consider the local company pension scheme. Indeed, you may have no choice if membership of the company scheme is a condition of employment, as it often used to be in the UK until 1988. However, membership should entitle you to receive employer contributions and all the tax reliefs associated with locally approved pension arrangements. The downside is that you may have to work for several years to meet the minimum qualifying period for a pension and, even if you do, for legal reasons it may not be possible to transfer your benefits out of the country when you leave.

Tax problems

Taxation is the main stumbling block in any expatriate pension package, and even if you remain in the UK scheme you may hit problems. Currently the European Commission is looking at ways to make it easier to remain in your home country scheme. This should eliminate certain problems – for example, many foreign tax authorities will treat an expatriate's pension contributions paid by the UK employer to the UK scheme as extra income and will tax them accordingly.

If you do hit this problem, try to get compensation in your pay package for the extra tax levied. In practice, however, many companies maintain the pension promise but do not bother to fund it during the period the employee is abroad, particularly where this is for a short period. In other words, they guarantee the pension, but do not set aside specific contributions to cover that guarantee. No employer contributions, no tax penalty in the country of assignment.

When the employee returns to the UK and rejoins the UK company's scheme, the Revenue will allow pension provision for all the years in service, including the overseas secondment, provided the maximum pension is in line with what would have been earned if the employee had stayed in the UK. The notional UK salary can take account of promotions and inflation. After ten years the Revenue would normally insist that you leave the scheme, but even this may be negotiable by your employer.

Offshore trusts

Offshore pension trusts can be an effective and tax-efficient way of providing pension benefits for senior executives, particularly where the peripatetic nature of their career makes it impossible for them to remain within the UK company scheme.

The trust, often sited in the Channel Islands, can be designed to provide higher benefits and earlier retirement than the main UK company scheme. Where you plan to retire abroad the trust can even be set up to pay your pension in a different currency.

It sounds ideal, but be careful if you are offered something along these lines. Offshore trusts are complex and must be arranged by a reputable firm of employee benefits consultants and legal experts. Any arrangement should be backed by formal documentation and this should be checked by your own accountant or legal and tax adviser, provided they have expertise in this area. There can be all sorts of problems, for example hidden tax charges, if you bring the fund back into the UK.

Offshore plans

An increasing number of financial institutions sell long-term investment plans to expatriates from the Channel Islands, the Isle of Man, Dublin and other offshore centres. Some of these are designed to mirror pension plans in the UK, but they should not be confused with the genuine article because they cannot mirror the tax advantages of an onshore, Revenue-approved plan. However, some offer limited tax advantages, and it may be possible to transfer to a UK plan if you return home.

If you think this might be your only option, watch out for high charges and sales commissions. Also, check that the contract does not lock you in to a fixed period of contribution. If your secondment is cut short and you return to the UK, you could face punitive early termination penalties.

> If your secondment is cut short and you return to the UK, you could face punitive early termination penalties.

Be sure to consult an independent financial adviser who specializes in offshore products and in expatriate tax and pension planning. Make sure the adviser will also consider the wide range of offshore investment funds (similar to unit trust and unit-linked funds in the UK). These may provide better long-term growth prospects and prove more flexible than some of the insurance products.

Retiring abroad

Your first financial consideration if you plan to retire abroad is to arrange for all your pensions and other sources of income to be paid abroad without double tax penalties. Expert advice on pension and inheritance tax planning is essential.

Claiming your state pension

The UK state pension is paid at age 65 for men, and between age 60 and 65 for women depending on when they retire. (The female state pension age is due to be raised in line with the male pension age, and there is a transition period between 2010 and 2020 to achieve this.)

According to the DSS, the state retirement pensions and widows' benefits can be claimed from anywhere in the world. However, annual cost of living increases are paid only if you live in a European Union country or a country with which Britain has a social security agreement which provides for uprating (see Table 23.1). This means that if you retire to Australia, Canada, New Zealand or any country not mentioned in the table, your state pension will be frozen either at the time you leave the UK or, for those already abroad when they reach state retirement age, at the time of the first payment.

Clearly, the loss of the annual cost of living increases will rapidly erode the value of the pension over a 15–20 year retirement, and extra income from other sources will be required to compensate. The only good news is that if you return to live in the UK, your state pension will be paid at the

Table 23.1 Countries where your state pension qualifies for the annual increase

Austria	Guernsey	Netherlands	Yugoslavia
Barbados	Iceland	Norway	(including
Belgium	Irish Republic	Philippines	the newly
Bermuda	Israel	Portugal	independent
Cyprus	Italy	Spain	former republics)
Denmark	Jamaica	Sweden	
Finland	Jersey	Switzerland	
France	Luxembourg	Turkey	
Germany	Malta	US	
Gibraltar	Mauritius		

Source: Department of Social Security

full current rate. UK expats on a temporary visit home can also claim the full rate, but only for the period spent in this country.

If you go abroad for short periods, the DSS makes special arrangements to pay your pension. No action is necessary where the period is less than three months, and in this case your pension payments can be collected on your return.

For periods between three and six months, you can arrange for your bank or building society to transfer payments to a bank overseas. For periods over six months, the DSS will, on request, pay a sterling cheque to an overseas bank. Alternatively you can collect the lump sum on your return. For over 12 months, a more permanent arrangement is made to pay your pension by automated credit transfer to your overseas bank. However, if you wish, you can leave the pension for up to a maximum of two years and collect the lump sum on your return.

Claiming your company or private pension

Company and private individual pensions can also be paid abroad. However, most statements that explain your future pension rights assume retirement is within the UK, so it is essential to check how retiring abroad will affect your tax position. For example, the tax-free cash lump sum that is an important feature of UK private pensions is not recognized in North America, and if you receive the benefit there it may be taxed along with the pension.

Also, remember that your pension will be subject to currency fluctuations. If the local currency in your retirement country rises against the pound, then the value of your UK pension will reduce in real terms. The places where you avoid exchange risk are those which use sterling, namely, the Isle of Man and Gibraltar and once we join the Euro, the Euro zone countries.

Pensions from previous employment

Many people change jobs several times before reaching retirement, so it will be necessary to contact previous employers to check the value of any benefits you left in the former employers' schemes. These benefits are known as 'deferred' pensions. Where a company has been taken over or become insolvent and it is difficult to track down the trustees, the Pensions Register will trace your benefits free of charge (contact The Occupational Pensions Regulatory Authority – the website address is in Appendix 2).

If your career included overseas employment with foreign state and company pension entitlements, the tracing problems could be multiplied ten-fold. To add to the complications, foreign pensions schemes may have a different retirement age from the rest of your UK pensions.

Taxation

Once you have checked your sources of pension, it is time to examine how they will be taxed. Expert advice is essential here, and clearly the adviser must be conversant with the tax and pensions rules in the country of retirement. The object of the exercise is to pay tax on pensions and investment income just once – usually in your country of retirement.

Where the country you choose has a double taxation agreement with the UK (there are more than 80 of these agreements in operation), the Inland Revenue will allow pensions to be paid gross. But first you will need a declaration from the foreign tax authorities stating that they are taxing you on your worldwide income.

This declaration should be sent immediately to your UK tax office. If there is a delay, your pensions will be taxed twice – once in the UK, at the basic rate of income tax, and again in your country of retirement. However, if there is a delay in sending the form, the Inland Revenue confirms that the withholding tax can be reclaimed when it receives the declaration from the foreign tax authority.

Summary

Working abroad

- Can you stay in your present company's scheme?
- Will the company guarantee that you will be no worse off than if you had remained in the UK?
- If there is no company scheme, consider a local pension arrangement, provided your expected period of employment will allow you to meet the minimum qualifying periods.
- If you look for an offshore pension, beware of the high charges associated with some of these plans and do not lock in to a long-term regular commitment.

Retiring abroad

- Find out whether your state pension will receive cost of living increases.
- Check the value of your UK company pensions using the Pensions Register to trace any benefits from former employment if necessary.
- Check the expected value of any individual pension plans.
- Trace any overseas pension benefits (state and private).
- Find out how your pensions will be taxed in the retirement country.

Further information

Ask at your local DSS office for leaflet NI 106, *Pensioners or Widows Going Abroad* and NI 38, *Social Security Abroad*.

For further information write to: Department of Social Security, Overseas Benefits Directorate, Payments Group, Longbenton, Newcastle upon Tyne NE98 1YX. The DSS website is at ***www.dss.gov.uk***.

Bluffers' guide to jargon

Accrual rate: The rate at which a pension scheme member's pension rights build up. In a 'sixtieths' scheme your pension would build up at a rate of 1/60 of your final salary for each year of service. In this case it would take 40 years to build up the maximum pension allowed by the Inland Revenue of 40/60 or two-thirds of final salary (subject to restrictions in the case of some higher earners – see *earnings cap*).

Accumulation unit: Units in a unit trust where the income generated is re-invested automatically, increasing the unit price. The alternative is *income units* where the income is distributed to the unitholders.

Active investment management: Active managers use in-house and external research, together with their own detailed knowledge of companies and their management teams, in order to actively select the stocks. See *passive investment management*.

Added years: Where the pension is expressed as a proportion of final salary, typically it will build up at the rate of 1/60 of final salary for each year of service. Some *additional voluntary contributions (AVC)* schemes allow members to top up their main pension scheme benefits by investing to build up extra 'years'.

Additional voluntary contributions (AVCs): Extra contributions to a separate fund paid by the member in addition to the main scheme contributions. Total employee contributions to the main scheme and AVC combined must not exceed 15 per cent of annual earnings. AVCs are normally run by insurance companies, building societies and, occasionally, unit trust groups. See also *free-standing additional voluntary contributions*, *stakeholder schemes* and *individual savings accounts*.

Advisory management: An advisory investment management service means that you may discuss investment opportunities with your manager but no action can be taken without your approval.

Annual charge: The annual management charge made by your investment manager.

Annuity: An annuity provides a guaranteed income, usually for life, in return for a lump sum investment. With an investment-linked annuity your income will be dictated partly by stock market returns.

Appointed representative: Companies that have a contract with a life office to sell one or more of its products on an exclusive basis in return for a commission payment.

Appropriate personal pension: Introduced in 1988, the appropriate personal pension allows employees who are not members of a 'contracted out' company pension scheme to contract out of *Serps* on an individual basis in return for a rebate of National Insurance contributions which are invested in your chosen plan.

Assets: A catch-all phrase which refers to the sectors in which funds invest, for example UK equities, European Union equities and fixed-interest securities (bonds).

Association of Investment Trust Companies (AITC): The main trade body for investment trusts.

Association of Unit Trust and Investment Funds (AUTIF): The main trade body for unit trusts and open-ended investment companies.

Authorized unit trusts: Unit trusts sold to the public must be authorized by the Financial Services Authority (FSA), the chief regulator for financial services in the UK.

Band earnings: National Insurance for employees is levied on what are known as 'band earnings', that is earnings between lower and upper limits (known as the lower earnings limit or LEL and the upper earnings limit or UEL). These are £87 and £575 per week for the 2001–2002 tax year.

Basic state pension: The basic or 'old age' pension is a flat-rate benefit paid to individuals who reach state pension age and have paid or been credited with sufficient National Insurance contributions during their working life.

Bed and spouse: At the end of the tax year it is common practice to sell shares and for your spouse or partner to re-purchase them the following day in order to crystallize a capital gain or loss to use in conjunction with the annual capital gains tax exemption (£7,500 in 2001–2002).

Beneficiaries: Literally, those who benefit from a trust. With a unit trust, the trustees run the fund on behalf of the beneficiaries – in this case the unitholders. With a pension fund, the beneficiaries are the scheme members and their dependants.

Bid price: The price at which you sell units in a unit trust back to the investment manager. You purchase at the *offer price*.

Bid/offer spread: The full initial cost of your investment in a fund. This includes administration, sales commission if applicable, dealing costs and stamp duty among other items. Typically, the spread is about 5–6 per cent, but where the initial charge is reduced or abolished it could be as low as 0.5 per cent.

Bond: UK bonds are issued by borrowers – for example the government and companies – which undertake to repay the principal sum on a specified date, rather like an IOU. During the time the bond is outstanding a fixed rate of interest is paid to the lender. Not to be confused with insurance bonds which are collective investments sold by insurance companies.

Capital gains tax (CGT): The tax on the increase in the value of an asset when it is sold, compared with its value at the time of purchase, adjusted partly to take account of inflation and partly according to the length of time you have held the asset. See *taper relief*.

Capital growth: An increase in the value of shares or assets in a fund.

Carry back: A special pension provision exists for employees and the self-employed who have unused tax relief in the previous tax year to ask the Inland Revenue to treat a contribution you are making now as if it had been paid in the previous tax year.

Commission: 1. On the sale of an investment or insurance product the management company may pay a financial adviser a commission. 2. The fee that a stockbroker may charge clients for dealing on their behalf.

Commutation: See *tax-free cash*.

Company representative: Also known as direct salesman and tied agent. Company representatives are employed directly by the life office and work solely for that company.

Contracted out/contracted in: Most company pension schemes in the UK are 'contracted out' of the state earnings-related pension scheme (*Serps*) and pay a reduced rate of employee and employer National

Insurance contributions. The difference between the full and reduced rate contribution is invested to provide a level of pension which broadly matches what members would have got under Serps.

Contract note: Confirmation of your share purchase.

Contribution limits: The Inland Revenue sets out maximum contributions that an individual can pay each year. In a company scheme employees can pay up to 15 per cent of 'pensionable pay', while in a personal pension, the limit is between 17.5 – 40 per cent of 'net relevant earnings', depending on age. The employer's contributions are not restricted under a company scheme but are included under the personal pension limits. See *stakeholder pension schemes*.

Convertibles: Fixed-interest securities which may be converted to equities at some future date.

Corporate bond: An IOU issued by a public company. See *bond*.

Coupon: The rate of interest paid by a bond or gilt.

Custodian: Usually a bank, whose primary function is to look after a fund's assets.

Death in retirement benefits: The pension and lump sum paid to the deceased member's spouse and/or other dependants where death occurs in retirement.

Death in service benefits: The pension and lump sum paid to the deceased member's spouse and/or other dependants where death occurs while still employed.

Debentures: Bonds issued by UK companies which are secured on the company's underlying assets – for example, property. Unsecured bonds are known as 'loan stocks'.

Deferred pensioner: A scheme member who changes employment and leaves behind his or her pension benefits. The benefits are known as a deferred pension because the pension is held by the scheme until retirement age.

Deficit: In pension fund terms, a deficit is identified when the fund cannot meet its liabilities – the guaranteed benefits it must pay.

Defined benefit: A US term for *final salary scheme*. This is a pension scheme which links your pension to your salary, usually at or just before retirement. Generally there is no direct link between what you pay in and the emerging pension.

Defined contribution: This refers to money purchase pensions, where there is no direct link between the pension and your salary at retirement. Instead your contributions build up a fund by an annuity.

Dependants: In the context of a pension scheme, the members' or beneficiaries' dependants are usually limited to the spouse and children under 18.

Derivative: Financial instruments are referred to as 'derivative securities' when their value is dependent upon the value of some other underlying asset. The value of the derivative security is derived from the value of the underlying security. See *future*, *option* and *warrant*.

Designated account: An account held in one name (often a child's) with a second name as additional identification.

Discount: If the share price of an investment trust is lower than the value per share of the underlying assets, the difference is known as the 'discount'. If it is higher, the difference is known as the 'premium'. As a general rule, a share trading at a discount represents good value.

Discretionary benefits: Non-guaranteed benefits, although in some cases they can become an expectation – typically, where pension increases above the guaranteed minimum are paid on a regular basis. Discretionary payments are paid at the 'discretion' of the trustees. The trust deed and rules, for example, may include a 'discretion' to allow trustees to pay death benefits and spouse's pensions to common law partners.

Discretionary management: An investment service where you give your manager total control over the day-to-day running of your portfolio or units. The manager makes all the investment decisions.

Distributions: Income paid out from an equity or bond fund.

Dividend: The owner of shares is entitled to dividends – the annual or six-monthly distribution to shareholders of part of the company's profits.

Dividend yield: See *gross yield*.

Earnings cap: Introduced in the 1989 Budget, the cap restricts the amount of salary on which pension contributions and benefits are based. For the 2001–2002 tax year, the earnings cap is £95,400.

Employee share schemes: A range of schemes that offer you the chance to buy shares in your employer's company at a discount.

Enterprise investment scheme (EIS): Available by direct subscription. EISs offer a range of tax reliefs if you invest in the shares of mainly unquoted trading companies.

Enterprise zone trust (EZT): Available by direct subscription. EZTs are designated areas where tax reliefs and reduced administrative controls are used to attract new business, providing investment in property with income tax relief on most of the cost.

Equities: The ordinary share capital of a company.

Eurosterling bond: A corporate bond issued in pounds sterling by a company which wants to borrow money on the international markets rather than just in the UK.

Ex-dividend: The period of about six weeks before a fund or equity pays out its dividend/income. If you buy during this period, you are not entitled to that dividend.

Execution-only: With this type of service, the investment manager/ stockbroker simply buys and sells at your request without offering any advice.

Exit charge: A charge deducted from certain funds if you pull out early – usually within the first five years.

Fee-based adviser: Many firms of financial advisers do not accept sales commission. Instead they charge a fee calculated on an hourly basis, or occasionally on a per case basis. This means that the adviser's remuneration is not dependent on the sale of financial products.

Final salary scheme: Final salary schemes (in the US known as 'defined benefit' schemes) link the value of the pension to earnings, usually in the few years leading to retirement. Typically the pension builds up at a rate of 1/60 of final salary for each year of service up to a maximum of 40/60 or two-thirds final salary (subject to restrictions in the case of certain higher earners – see *earnings cap*). See *money purchase*.

Financial Services Act 1986: The Act which set up the system of regulation for financial services.

Financial Services Authority: The FSA is the chief regulator under the Act.

Fixed-interest security: Another term for bonds. See *bond*, *corporate bond*.

FTSE 100 Index: The index which covers the top 100 companies on the UK Stock Exchange measured by market capitalization (the number of shares times the share value).

FTSE All-Share Index: The index which measures the bulk of the companies listed on the UK Stock Exchange – about 770 in total.

FTSE Mid 250 Index: The index which measures the 250 companies below (by market capitalization) the FTSE 100.

Free-standing additional voluntary contributions (FSAVCs): If your company pension is likely to fall short of the maximum two-thirds final salary set by the Revenue, it is possible to pay voluntary top-up contributions either to the company *additional voluntary contribution* (AVC) scheme or to an individual plan called a free-standing AVC. You can also use a *stakeholder* or *personal pension* in some circumstances.

Fund of funds: A unit trust which can only invest in other authorized unit trusts.

Funded and unfunded unapproved schemes: These are pension schemes recognized by the Revenue but not approved for tax purposes. They are used to provide pensions for employees caught by the *earnings cap*.

Future: A type of *derivative*. A futures contract is a legally binding agreement to buy or sell an amount of shares (or other instruments) at a fixed date in the future at a fixed price.

Gearing: The relationship between debt and assets. High gearing means that there is a large proportion of debt in relation to the assets held. *Investment trusts* can borrow to invest in assets, unit trusts can do so only to a limited extent.

Gilt: The most secure type of *bond* because they are issued by the UK government.

Gross yield: This is a method of assessing the income from an investment. It is the annual gross dividend expressed as a percentage of the current market price. This shows the rate of gross income return a shareholder would receive on an investment at the share price on the date specified – much as one might describe the interest received on a deposit account. The important point to note is that for equities, investment trusts and equity-based unit trusts held within an Isa, the yield is paid net. The Isa manager reclaims the tax.

Group personal pension (GPP): This is little more than a series of individual personal pension plans, although if the employer sets up the group plan he is more likely to make a contribution and, perhaps, provide life assurance and other benefits on top. The GPP is not defined as an occupational scheme and so the same contribution and benefit limits as individual personal pensions apply.

Guaranteed equity funds: Funds which limit your exposure to falls in the stock market and provide a percentage of the gains. They do this by investing mainly in gilts and cash and then buying derivatives to provide the guarantees.

Hedge funds: Funds which aim to provide 'absolute returns' – that is positive returns throughout all market cycles.

Income drawdown: Rather than immediately purchase an annuity at retirement, with a drawdown plan you can draw an income while keeping the rest of your pension fund fully invested up to age 75 at the latest.

Income unit: If you buy income units in a unit trust, you receive automatically your share of the income generated by the fund. However, you can opt to have the income re-invested within the fund. Compare with *accumulation units*, where the dividends are re-invested to increase the unit price.

Independent financial adviser: IFAs, as they are known in the trade, are not tied to any one life office, but instead search the market to find the best product for your needs.

Index tracking: With a tracker fund, the investment manager uses a computer model to select stocks to simulate the performance of a specific stock market index. Index tracking is also known as 'passive management'. The alternative is 'active management' where the manager selects individual stocks on the basis of research into a company's prospects in the light of expected economic conditions.

Individual savings account (Isa): The Isa replaced Peps and Tessas in April 1999 as the main tax-efficient investment after pensions.

Inheritance tax: A tax on wealth passed on at death. The nil rate band is £242,000 in 2001–2002. Anything over this is taxed at 40 per cent, although gifts between husband and wife are exempt.

Inherited Serps: If your spouse dies after October 2002 before reaching state retirement age, you will receive only 50 per cent of his/her Serps pension. Previously this was 100 per cent.

Initial charge: A charge, typically 5 per cent, levied by the investment manager to cover administration and sales commission when you invest in a fund. However, the full upfront cost of your investment is shown in the *bid/offer spread*, which includes additional charges such as stamp duty.

Integration: Company pension schemes that are integrated with the basic state pension scheme do not provide a pension for the first slice of earnings up to the lower earnings limit for *National Insurance*.

Investment trust: A UK company, listed on the stock exchange, which invests in the shares of other companies in the UK and overseas. Investment trust companies have a fixed number of shares which are subject to the usual market forces, so the share price does not necessarily reflect the underlying net asset value. See *discount* and *premium*.

Key features document: The (supposedly) simple summary you receive about a product before you sign up. The most important feature is the details on charges, but it should also include details on the risk level of the investment and the pattern of contributions to which you are committed.

Life assurance: This provides a tax free lump sum if you die during the insured period.

Life office: A life assurance company authorized to sell life and pensions products. The term is also used to describe the life assurance arm of a composite insurer. Composites sell life and pensions products, and also general insurance such as household and motor cover.

Loan stocks: Unsecured bonds issued by UK companies. Bonds secured on a company's underlying assets (property, for example) are known as debentures. See *bonds*.

Lower earnings limit: The threshold above which you pay National Insurance contributions – up to the upper earnings limit. The lower limit is £87 per week and the upper limit is £575 per week.

Managed/mixed fund: This is a broadly diversified fund which invests in a range of the manager's other main funds, usually including UK and overseas equities, gilts, bonds and, in some cases, property.

Market maker: A dealer who can buy and sell shares.

Married woman's stamp: More correctly, the 'reduced' rate of National Insurance contribution women can still pay provided they were married or widowed before April 5, 1977. The reduced rate does not build up an entitlement to the basic state pension, among other benefits.

Minimum Income Guarantee (MIG): This guarantees a minimum weekly benefit to very low-income pensioners. The MIG, paid through Income Support, tops up the basic pension to £92.15 in 2001–2002.

Money purchase: Money purchase or *defined contribution* schemes do not guarantee a pension linked to the member's final salary. Instead, contributions are invested to build up a fund which is used at retirement to buy an annuity from a life office. The annuity provides the guaranteed regular income until death. See *annuity*.

Mutual life office: A mutual life office is effectively owned by its policyholders and, unlike a 'proprietary' company, it does not have shareholders.

National Insurance: A form of taxation levied on 'band' earnings – that is earnings between the lower and upper earnings limits (see *lower earnings limit*). These are £87 and £575 per week for the 2001–2002 tax year.

National Insurance rebate: A portion of National Insurance contributions is rebated to individuals who contract out of the state earnings-related pension scheme with an appropriate personal pension. See *Serps*.

National Savings certificates: Available direct from National Savings or via the Post Office. NS certificates offer a tax-free return.

Net asset value (NAV): The market value of an *investment trust*'s underlying assets. This may be different from the share price since the latter is subject to market forces and supply and demand. See *discount* and *premium*.

Net relevant earnings: Earnings on which personal pension contributions are based.

Net yield: The return on an investment after tax has been deducted. See *gross yield*.

Occupational Pension Regulatory Authority (OPRA): This is the regulator for company pensions, established under the Pensions Act 1995. It took over from the Occupational Pensions Board in April 1997. OPRA maintains a register of *stakeholder* providers.

Occupational pension scheme: A scheme sponsored by an employer to provide relevant benefits to employees.

Occupational Pensions Advisory Service (OPAS): Provides a free
service to pension scheme members, pensioners, deferred pensioners
and their dependants who have a complaint about their scheme.

Offer price: The price at which you buy units from the unit trust or Isa
manager. You sell back to the manager at the *bid price*.

Open market option: Your right at retirement to take the proceeds of
your personal pension (or similar) and buy your annuity elsewhere.
Annuity rates (the income you buy with your pension fund) vary
considerably so it is vital to shop around.

Option: A type of *derivative*. A call option gives the buyer the right (but
not the obligation, hence 'option') to buy a commodity, stock, bond or
currency in the future at a mutually agreed price struck on the date of
the contract. Put options give you the right, but not the obligation, to
sell.

Oeics: Open-ended investment companies are a type of investment fund.
They are similar to unit trusts, but have a corporate structure, and so
are not based on a trust. They have a single price rather than a
bid/offer spread.

Passive investment management: Another term for *index tracking*.

Pension age: The age at which you can draw your pension from the
state scheme, your company scheme or your individual plan.

Pension forecast: A useful service provided by the Department of Social
Security which tells you what your state pension is worth.

Pensions: Available from a range of financial institutions, and also
provided by many employers in the form of an occupational pension
scheme. Pension schemes and plans approved by the Inland Revenue
offer tax relief on contributions, tax-free growth of the fund and, in
some cases, a tax-free lump sum at retirement. The pension income is
taxed.

Pensions ombudsman: An independent arbitrator for pension disputes
– usually referred by *OPAS*. The ombudsman has statutory power to
enforce his decisions.

Performance measurement: Used to check how well or badly the
investment manager has done. There are usually two measurements:
first, against an industry average; and second, against a specific sector
of similar funds.

Personal equity plan (Pep): A Pep is a wrapper or basket which shelters Inland Revenue-approved stock market investments from the taxman. It was replaced by *Individual savings accounts* in 1999 but existing funds can be kept in the Pep wrappers.

Personal Investment Authority (PIA): Now part of the Financial Services Authority. Under the Financial Services Act 1986, the PIA was the regulator for companies which market and sell retail investments such as pensions and life assurance savings plans.

Pooled funds: Another term for collective or mutual funds which invest in a range of shares and other instruments to achieve diversification and economies of scale for the smaller investor who buys units in these funds.

Preference share (pref): This is similar to a *bond* in that it pays a fixed rate of interest, although its payment depends on company profits. Preference shares are first in the pecking order of payouts when an investment trust is wound up. See *stepped preference share* and *zero dividend preference share*.

Premium: If the share price of an investment trust is higher than the value of the underlying assets, the difference is known as the premium. Normally, investors are advised not to buy under these circumstances. If the price is lower than the *net asset value* (NAV) the difference is known as the *discount*.

Price earnings ratio: The market price of a share divided by the company's earnings (profits) per share in its latest 12-month trading period.

Property: In the context of pension fund investment, property means the ownership of land and buildings that are used by businesses or other organizations which pay rent to the owner. Ownership is often on a collective basis.

Proprietary life office: Proprietary life offices are quoted companies and have shareholders, unlike 'mutual' life offices which are effectively owned by their policyholders.

Protected rights: The fund which is built up from the rebates of National Insurance contributions under a personal pension and other types of money purchase pensions. See *money purchase*.

Purchased life annuity (PLA): See *annuity*.

Qualifying year: A complete tax year in which the full rate of National Insurance contribution was paid or credited. Qualifying years count towards your basic state pension.

Redemption: The date at which a *bond* becomes repayable.

Redemption yield: The current dividend or interest rate increased or decreased to take into account the capital value if the bond is held to maturity.

Renewal commission: Often overlooked by the consumer, the renewal commission is paid by the life office to the adviser annually from year two throughout the contract. Also known as *trailer commission*.

Retirement annuity: Retirement annuity contracts were the predecessors of personal pensions, and were similar in most respects except that they did not allow individual employees to contract out of Serps.

Return: The amount by which your investment increases as a result of interest or dividend income and capital growth.

Risk: A measure of the probability that the value of your savings and the income they generate will fall as well as rise.

Running yield: The current dividend or interest payments on a fund.

Scrip issue/dividends: A scrip issue is where a company turns part of its accumulated reserves into new shares. Scrip dividends cannot be put in an Isa because they do not carry a tax credit, so you cannot reclaim the tax.

Securities: The general name for all stocks and shares. Broadly speaking, stocks are fixed-interest securities and shares are the rest. The four main types of securities listed and traded on the UK Stock Exchange are UK equities, overseas equities (i.e. issued by non-UK companies), UK gilts (bonds issued by the UK government) and bonds/fixed-interest stocks (issued by companies and local authorities).

Self-invested personal pensions (SIPPs): These are similar to personal pensions, but allow the individual to separate the administration and investment, and therefore allow the individual to exercise much greater freedom in the investment choice. Only viable for larger investments.

Self-select Isa: A plan which does not restrict you to the funds of one Isa manager but instead allows you to hold the entire range of permitted assets, including individual shares and bonds as well as unit and investment trusts.

Serps: The state earnings-related pension scheme was set up in 1978 to provide employees with a pension linked to average earnings between the lower and upper threshold for *National Insurance*. It is being phased out.

Single premium/recurring single premium (SP/RSP): A one-off contribution that does not lock you in to any future payments. If commission is paid to the adviser, this also is on a one-off basis, so there are no financial penalties if you decide not to pay further contributions. Recurring single premiums should be treated as one-off payments for commission purposes, but do check this point.

Size-weighted average: The average return after weighting each company in the index by size of market capitalization at the start of the period. This means that the performance of really small shares or trusts does not have a disproportionate impact on an index. Size-weighted average is the preferred method used by the independent measurers of the big institutional pension funds.

Small self-administered schemes (SSASs): Approved occupational pension schemes for small businesses which allow far more flexibility than standard schemes. For example, they include the facility to self-invest to a high degree, and to take a loan from the fund. The maximum number of members is 12.

Split-capital trust: An *investment trust* which has different types of shares – for example, some offer a high income but no capital growth, and some offer pure capital growth but no income.

Stakeholder pension schemes: These were launched in April 2001. A stakeholder is a type of *personal pension* which must offer low-cost, low minimum premiums and penalty-free entry and exit terms. Anyone under the age of 75 can pay £3,600 per annum to a stakeholder irrespective of earnings. Employees in company schemes who earn less than £30,000 can also take out a stakeholder or standard personal pension and pay up to £3,600 per annum in addition to the company scheme contributions.

Stamp duty: A tax on the purchase (but not the sale) of shares, currently 0.5 per cent.

Stepped preference share: Stepped preference shares are shares in a *split-capital trust* which pay dividends that rise at a predetermined rate and have a fixed redemption value, paid when the trust is wound up.

Stock market indices: An index is a specified basket or portfolio of shares and shows how these share prices are moving in order to give an indication of market trends. Every major world stock market is represented by at least one index. The *FTSE 100 Index*, for example, reflects the movements of the share prices of the UK's largest 100 quoted companies by market capitalization.

Taper relief: Reduces the capital gains tax liability according to the length of time you have held an asset before you sell.

Tax-exempt special savings accounts (Tessas): Replaced by cash *individual savings accounts* in April 1999.

Tax-free cash: Under Inland Revenue rules, it is possible to take part of your pension benefits at retirement in the form of tax-free cash. This process is known as 'commutation'.

Tax year: Tax and investment allowances apply to the 12 months from April 6 to the following April 5.

Tracker funds: See *index tracking*.

Trailer commission: See *renewal commission*.

Transfer value: The amount you take out of a pension scheme if you leave employment and want to transfer your pension benefits into the new employer's scheme or into an individual pension plan.

Trust deed: The legal document on which a unit trust is based. The use of a trust separates the fund from the management company's assets. The trustees manage the fund on behalf of the beneficiaries – in this case, the unitholders.

Trustee: You can't have a trust without a trustee who, as legal owner of the fund, looks after the assets on behalf of the unitholders.

Unapproved pension schemes: Schemes that are recognized by the Revenue, but are not approved for tax purposes. Used mainly to top up benefits for employees caught by the *earnings cap*. See *funded and unfunded unapproved schemes*.

Upper earnings limit: See *National Insurance*.

Voluntary benefits: Insurance products and other items offered by your employer at a discount to the individual retail price.

Waiver of premium: With a regular premium pension plan, if you have this feature the pension company credits your fund with contributions under certain circumstances – for example if you are too ill to work.

Warrant: Risky and volatile investments which give the holder the right but not the obligation to buy investment trust shares at a predetermined price within a specified period. This type of share has no voting rights and holders do not normally receive dividends.

Winding up: The term used to explain the legal termination of a pension scheme. Details on how the scheme should be wound up are set out in the trust deed and rules.

'With profits': With profits funds are invested in UK and overseas equities, gilts, bonds and property. Under a with profits contract, the life office provides a guaranteed minimum sum at maturity, to which it adds annual or 'reversionary' bonuses which, once allocated, cannot be taken away. The annual bonuses are 'smoothed' to avoid volatility. On top of this, there is a discretionary (not guaranteed) final 'terminal' bonus which reflects recent performance of the with profits fund.

Yield: The annual dividend or income on an investment expressed as a percentage of the purchase price. See *gross yield*.

Zero dividend preference share ('zero'): A lower-risk and predetermined investment. It offers a fixed-capital return in the form of a redemption value which is paid when the trust is wound up. These shares are not entitled to income, and therefore there is no income tax liability.

Financial planning, investment advisers and a guide to making complaints

Before you appoint a firm to act on your behalf, you can check with the chief regulator, the Financial Services Authority, that the firm is authorized and registered with the appropriate regulator. To contact the **FSA central register**, phone 020 7929 3652, website *www.fsa.gov.uk*.

Stockbrokers and investment managers

The Association of Private Client Investment Managers and Stockbrokers publishes a free directory of member firms, many of which provide a full financial planning service. Contact APCIMS, 112 Middlesex Street, London E1 7HY. The APCIMS directory is available at *www.apcims.co.uk*. E-mail *info@apcims.co.uk*.

Financial planners and advisers

The Institute of Financial Planning is multi-disciplinary and its members are well qualified in giving independent planning advice. Contact the IFP at Whitefriars Centre, Lewins Mead, Bristol BS1 2NT. For the register of fellows of the institute, phone 0117 930 4434 or go to *www.financialplanning.org.uk*.

The Society of Financial Advisers is part of the Chartered Insurance Institute and is a major examiner of independent advisers and life assurance company sales staff. Contact SOFA at 20 Aldermanbury, London EC2V 7HY. Tel: 020 7417 4419. *www.sofa.org.uk*.

Independent advisers: For a list of three local independent advisers, contact **IFA Promotion** on 0117 971 1177 or at *www.ifap.org.uk*. For fee-based independent advisers, contact the **Money Management Register** on 0117 976 9444.

Accountants

About 700 members of the Institute of Chartered Accountants are qualified to offer a full advisory service, but members of other taxation bodies can also help.

The Institute of Chartered Accountants in England & Wales, Moorgate Place, London EC2P 2BJ. Tel: 020 7920 8100/8711. *www.iceaw.co.uk*.

The Institute of Chartered Accountants in Scotland, 27 Queen Street, Edinburgh EH2 1LA. Tel: 0131 225 5673.

The Association of Chartered Certified Accountants (ACCA), 29 Lincoln's Inn Fields, London WC2A 3EE. Tel: 020 7242 6855. *www.acca.org.uk*.

The Chartered Institute of Taxation and Association of Tax Technicians, 12 Upper Belgrave Street, London SW1X 8BB. Chartered tax advisers and members of this institute specialize purely in tax work for companies and for individuals. Tel: 020 7235 9381. *www.tax.org.uk*.

Solicitors

The Law Society of England & Wales, 113 Chancery Lane, London WC2A 1PL. Tel: 020 7242 1222. *www.lawsociety.org.uk*

The Law Society of Scotland, 26 Drumsheugh Gardens, Edinburgh EH3 7YR. Tel: 0131 226 7411.

The Law Society of Northern Ireland, Law Society House, 98 Victoria Street, Belfast BT1 3JZ. Tel: 01232 231 614.

Solicitors are strongly represented in the financial services market. Two organizations dedicated to professional independent advice are:

Solicitors for Independent Financial Advice (SIFA): phone the helpline 01372 721172 or go to *www.solicitor-ifa.co.uk*.

The Association of Solicitor Investment Managers (ASIM), Chiddingstone Causeway, Tonbridge, Kent TN11 8JX. Tel: 01892 870065. *www.asim.org.uk*.

Pension specialists

The Association of Consulting Actuaries: Number 1 Wardrobe Place, London EC4V 5AH. Tel: 020 7248 3163. *www.aca.org.uk*.

Association of Pension Lawyers: APL, c/o Eversheds, Senator House, 65 Queen Victoria Street, London EC4V 4JA. Tel: 020 7919 4500.

Other useful organizations

Association of Investment Trust Companies: The AITC publishes a range of booklets on how to use investment trusts for long-term investment plans. AITC, Durrant House, 8–13 Chiswell Street, London EC1Y 4YY. Tel: 020 7431 5222. *www.aitc.org.uk*.

The Association of Unit Trusts and Investment Funds: AUTIF publishes a range of free fact sheets that explain how these investments work. AUTIF, 65 Kingsway, London WC2B 6TD. Tel: 020 7831 0898. *www.investmentfunds.org.uk*.

The Department of Social Security has a wealth of information on its website: *www.dss.gov.uk*.

The Occupational Pensions Regulatory Authority (Opra) runs the stakeholder scheme register. *www.opra.gov.uk*.

ProShare publishes a useful guide to employee share ownership. Contact ProShare, Library Chambers, 13–14 Basinghall Street, London EC2V 5BQ. Tel: 020 7220 1730. The website covers all the main arrangements and is at *www.proshare.org*.

The Stock Exchange publishes useful leaflets on buying and selling shares and on rolling settlement and nominee accounts. The Stock Exchange, London EC2N 1HP. Tel: 020 7797 1000. *www.londonstockexchange.com*.

Complaints

Under the Financial Services Act, if a company has sold you an inappropriate product for your needs you may be able to claim compensation.

If you have an investment complaint, write to the compliance officer at the company that sold you the product. You should receive an acknowledgement of your letter within seven days, but allow two months for the actual investigation before taking the case to the ombudsman or regulator.

The company's letterhead should show the details of the regulator but if not, contact the Financial Services Authority central register (see above) or write to: **The Financial Services Authority**, 25 The North Colonnade,

Canary Wharf, London E14 5HS. Consumer helpline: 0845 6061234. The FSA publishes a wide range of information leaflets on financial advice, pensions, investments and complaints. *www.fsa.gov.uk*.

The Financial Ombudsman Service is on 020 7964 1000.

Internet services and recommended reading

The internet

This section does not set out to provide a complete guide to Internet services but merely offers some tips on where to start. One of the best guides to online services is *e-cash* by Marianne Curphey (£10, published by Prentice Hall). This includes a run-down on the main online trading and information services. Marianne runs The Guardian Unlimited Money site at *www.guardian.co.uk*.

Fund prices and information

For collective funds, *www.iii.co.uk* lists total expense ratios (TERs) which add up all the charges, fees and costs incurred by managers to give you a more complete picture of the total cost than you will find in marketing literature. For information about funds and their performance try:

Trustnet *www.trustnet.co.uk*

Micropal *www.micropal.com*

Standard and Poor's *www.funds-sp.com*

A useful site for collective funds that includes details on the movement of star fund managers is *www.bestinvest.co.uk*.

Fund supermarkets

These are largely designed for individual savings accounts (see Chapter 12) as they allow you to mix and match funds from different managers within a single Isa. Some offer a limited selection of funds. Bear in mind that investment trusts are not well represented on these sites:

Fundnetwork *www.fidelity.co.uk*

Egg *www.egg.com*

FundsDirect *www.fundsdirect.co.uk*

Interactive Investor *www.iii.co.uk*

Tqonline *www.tqonline.co.uk*

Sharedealing

A comprehensive guide for the dedicated online trader is *The UK Guide to Online Brokers* by Michael Scott (Scott IT, 2000). There is an online version of the book at *www.investment-gateway.com*.

Many websites have share price charts, details of volume – that is how many people are trading a specific share at the time – and a portfolio tool that allows you to see how your shares are performing. There will be a time delay for most information, although this is usually just a matter of 15 minutes. Real-time prices for shares usually hold for 30 seconds while you decide whether or not to buy.

Once you have registered, opened an account and have a password, you can get access to the secure part of the site. The services are broadly similar but sites do try to differentiate themselves from the competition by including special features so it is worth visiting a few to see which suits you best.

If you are after an online stockbroker go to the APCIMS website which will help you search the register of members for this type of service. APCIMS is at *www.apcims.co.uk*. Several other services list online brokers and these include:

www.iii.co.uk

www.investorschronicle.co.uk

www.ftyourmoney.com

Information sites

The following information sites (some of which also offer dealing services) might be of interest but are not in any way intended as a recommendation:

BBC finance *www.bbc.co.uk/finance*

DLJdirect *www.dljdirect.co.uk*

E*Trade *www.etrade.co.uk*

Market Eye *www.marketeye.co.uk*

Hemmington Scott *www.hemscott.net*

Charles Schwab *www.schwab-worldwide.com*

UK-invest *www.ukinvest.co.uk*

Stockmarket news

Bloomberg *www.bloomberg.co.uk*

Financial Times *www.ft.com*

Yahoo! Finance *www.yahoo.co.uk/finance*

Portfolio construction

Useful information sites, which in certain cases provide information on how to construct a portfolio, include:

Motley Fool UK *www.fool.co.uk*

Interactive Investor *www.iii.co.uk*

UK Invest *www.ukinvest.co.uk*

Investors Chronicle *www.investorschronicle.com*

Recommended reading

A good source of reading matter is the ProShare website, which lists top publications and offers a discount on the retail price. Go to *www.proshare.org*.

Two books on interpreting financial pages in the *Financial Times* are *How to Read the Financial Pages* by Michael Brett, published by Random House, and *The Financial Times Guide to using the Financial Pages* by Romesh Vaitilingam, published by FT Prentice Hall.

For a good basic guide to investment, try *The Motley Fool UK Investment Guide*, published by Boxtree. Also excellent is Bernard Gray's *Beginners' Guide to Investment*, published by Century.

Finally, don't be without *The Investor's Guide to Information Sources*, published by ProShare.

Index